Living Through Dying
The Spiritual Experience of St Paul

Living Through Dying

The Spiritual Experience of St Paul

Revd D J Dales MA BD FRHistSoc

The Lutterworth Press
Cambridge

The Lutterworth Press
PO Box 60
Cambridge
CB1 2NT

British Library Cataloguing in Publication Data:
A catalogue record is available from the British Library.

ISBN: 0 7188 2898 4

Printed in Great Britain by The Bath Press

'Not only did crucifixion make possible the giving of the Spirit, but the life bestowed by the Spirit is a life of which crucifixion is a quality, a life of living through dying.'

(Michael Ramsey, *The Gospel and the Catholic Church*)

Contents

Foreword

When the Anglican Archbishop in Uganda, Janani Luwum, was murdered by order of General Idi Amin in 1977, there was an immediate sense that here was a man who had given his life for his faith, and for the church and people which he led. It was an authentic Christian martyrdom. Far away from Kampala, in the cathedral at Canterbury, the very stones of the building seemed to shudder in sympathetic understanding of the event. The people who lived and worked there felt directly in touch with the most famous moment in the history of that church, the murder in the cathedral of Archbishop Thomas Becket in 1170. The Dean and Chapter found themselves impelled to designate the easternmost chapel of the cathedral as the chapel of the saints and martyrs of the twentieth century. A representative group of men and women of our own time who had given their lives for their faith were named, coming not only from the churches of the Anglican communion, but from the three great families of Christendom: Catholic, Orthodox and Protestant.

The twentieth century has been, in a totally unexpected way, a century of Christian martyrdom. From different churches and different countries, confronted with different kinds of tyranny, Marxist or Fascist, and with military dictatorships of right and left, men and women have found themselves giving their lives for their faith. They have found in the most immediate and costly way the meaning of *Living Through Dying*. This book takes us back to the heart of that mystery which has been worked out in so many different circumstances. It tells us of the mystery of Christ and the Cross, above all, as it is expounded in the writings of St Paul. But it also looks at other of the earliest Christian writers, notably Ignatius of Antioch. As Douglas Dales says, 'The Cross and Christian participation in its redemptive suffering lie at the heart of all Ignatius' writing ... it is at the Cross that the union between God and man in Jesus is most fully revealed'. That union is one which links heaven and earth, time and eternity. As the present Patriarch of Antioch, Ignatius IV, says, 'The structure of history is *paschal* in the strict theological sense of 'passover', a passage from this present world into the new creation'.

In that passover all Christ's people are drawn together into one. If our twentieth century has been in any way a century of the renewal of Christian unity, that has been largely due to the hidden fact that this century has also been the time of the renewal of Christian martyrdom. It is one of the many virtues of this book that it illuminates that mysterious fact which is often overlooked and neglected, and in doing so enriches our understanding of the central themes of Christian faith and life.

The Revd Canon A. M. Allchin
February 1994

Preface

This book has been written with the needs of the churches in the English-speaking world very much in mind, especially those of the Anglican Communion and more particularly of the Church of England at the present time.

My sincere thanks are due firstly to my pupils at Marlborough College, whose kindness, interest and endless questions have elucidated many aspects of the gospel in its relationship to modern society. I am grateful too to my friends the clergy of the ecumenical parish of Marlborough and churches around who have welcomed me to share in the worship of the congregations which they serve. Thanks are also due to the Community of the Sisters of the Love of God and the Benedictine monks of Elmore Abbey for their prayers and encouragement; to Canon Donald Allchin for so kindly agreeing to contribute a foreword; to Colin Lester for his help as editor; and to those several Christian friends who have assisted in making the publication of this book a possibility.

Since the demise of Communism in the USSR my wife and I have been able to form many strong friendships with Christians in Latvia, Lithuania, Russia and Ukraine, among the Orthodox, Catholics, Lutherans and Old Believers. This book is a tribute to them and those whom they represent, living and departed, who on behalf of the worldwide church have passed through great travail on the road of living through dying, and from whom we have learnt so much.

Finally on a personal note, this book is dedicated to my beloved wife, with whom much of it has been discussed over a number of years. In the background is the living memory of two recent Anglican saints, Mother Mary Clare SLG and Archbishop Michael Ramsey, whose friendship, teaching and example bear out the words of St Paul to the church at Corinth: '*Quid autem habes quod non accepisti?*'

The Revd Douglas J. Dales
Marlborough, Advent 1993

Bibliographical note

The text of the Bible quoted, unless otherwise indicated, is that of the *Revised English Bible* (Oxford and Cambridge, 1989). The writings of the Apostolic Fathers are cited from the second edition (Leicester, 1989) of Lightfoot and Harmer, edited and revised by M. W. Holmes. The following works provide a wider context for this study, and a way into the extensive literature: *The Open Heaven*, by Christopher Rowland (London, 1982); *Meaning and Truth in II Corinthians*, by Frances Young and David Ford (London, 1987); *Dying, We Live*, by Kenneth Grayston (London, 1990); and *Paul and the Convert*, by Alan Segal (Newhaven and London, 1990).

D.J.D.

Preamble

St Paul is unique among the writers of the New Testament for the autobiographical testimony at the heart of his letters. However people react to him, there can be no doubt that the inner spiritual conflicts within Paul's personality are everywhere apparent. The conversion which began so dramatically upon the Damascus road proved to be a continuous process, and often a painful one, throughout the whole of his life. As a result much light is shed on what it meant for a Jewish Pharisee and rabbi to become a Christian. The severe conflict within Judaism induced by the preaching of Christ almost tore Paul apart. The inclusion of Gentiles within Christianity, but not within the Jewish Law, posed to early Jewish Christianity its most potent threat and challenge. Paul's life was a crucible in which the church was formed and its essential nature articulated.

At the same time Paul is the first among the Christian saints to express directly what it felt like to be 'in Christ', as he describes it so often. His own mission and ministry were literally driven by the Holy Spirit, often along hazardous and lonely paths. In his dialogue with other early Christian leaders he frequently found himself at loggerheads because of his loyalty to the vision of Christ as he had received it. Yet subsequent Christianity has affirmed the stand which he took; otherwise his letters would never have been so carefully collected and preserved, or regarded as authoritative and apostolic in nature. In the west his significance as a fount of systematic doctrine at the hands of St Augustine, and later still at those of Luther, has perhaps eclipsed his abiding role as a foremost spiritual father in the long tradition of Christian ascetic life and prayer. Yet frequently the language of Christian sanctity and spiritual testimony echoes with the ring of St Paul. The most striking example of this within the tradition of the British church is to be found in the *Confession* of St

Patrick, written in the early fifth century. The fusion of mission, suffering and vision is the same.

The content of the vision which Paul sought and encountered in Christ may be discerned in his writings as he tries to describe the indescribable 'glory of God in the face of Jesus Christ', and to explore its implications for Christian life and belief. He is therefore a mystic, a person whose whole life has been drawn to the threshold of eternity and is being transformed as a result. This mystical aspect of Paul's testimony is one of the reasons for his subsequent authority as a spiritual father. The essentially Jewish character of his mystical experience has recently been elucidated in a number of major studies of first-century Jewish apocalyptic mysticism. Paul emerges as a prime witness to the vitality and nature of this powerful tradition within Judaism. At the same time this tradition sheds invaluable light upon St Paul's testimony, and indeed upon the whole New Testament vision of Christ. For the writer of Hebrews asserts: 'the blood of Jesus makes us free to enter the sanctuary with confidence by the new and living way which Christ has opened for us ... the way of his flesh' (Heb. 10:19-20). What is unique about the visionary way in the New Testament is that it is the way of the Cross. The glory is discovered in the suffering.

In the two principal autobiographical passages of St Paul's writings, in Philippians 3 and 2 Corinthians, he sets forth the nature of this way of living through dying. Therein lies his unique authority as a spiritual guide. His insistence upon this way directly colours his whole theology as a Christian. All the main lines of his teaching – justification by faith; the indwelling of the Holy Spirit; the church as the Body of Christ; the tragedy of Israel's refusal of the Messiah; his eschatological vision; and his ethical teaching – are marked by the central experience of crucifixion-resurrection at the heart of Christian life as he knew it. His mysticism was genuinely apocalyptic in the sense that his vision was set upon the 'glory of God in the face of Jesus Christ', something to be sought after and apprehended as the true and present goal of earthly life. But the cost of this vision was ever deeper suffering, as Christ became formed in him through the spiritual conflict he encountered within and around him. This was his witness, his 'martyrdom', finally sealed by his death in Rome.

The purpose of this book is to examine in some detail the principal autobiographical passages, in order to hear as closely as possible what Paul is actually saying about his experience of living through dying. The manner of his testimony necessitates a fresh view of those passages in the Old Testament to which the earliest Christians turned in order to make sense both of the sufferings of Christ and of their own sufferings as his followers. The next generation of Christians after St Paul, the apostolic fathers, expound the meaning of the church's experience of persecution and death for the sake of Christ. This exposition heightens the appreciation of the force of St Paul's original witness to the fact that the place of suffering is the place of vision.

In this light, the nature and meaning of Paul's vision are examined in so far as they may be discerned in his writings. What was his experience of the resurrection life? How does he see things in the light of this vision? The final question will be the most urgent: what is the bearing of this vision for the life of our contemporary church today?

Chapter One

The way – I

"Who is equal to such a calling?"

Chapter 1

The way – I

At the heart of Paul's spiritual experience and evangelism lay a profound and permanent experience of entering into the dying of Christ. This was not just a matter of the manifold hardships which he experienced in the course of his apostolic ministry, as recorded in Acts and in his several letters. Rather it was that as he proclaimed the gospel by prayer, word and deed, he was assailed by deep suffering and the relentless hostility of evil. Although this often came by means of external suffering and afflictions, it was its inner spiritual impact that caused the deepest pain. Yet out of this experience Paul perceived the life and power of God at work, creating and sustaining the church, and enabling him to proclaim the reality of the resurrection with astonishing conviction and clarity. Central to this whole travail was Paul's own sense of the immediacy of Christ, and the strength of his personal relationship with him.

The most succinct summary of Paul's vision is given in Philippians 3. He lists his own impeccable inheritance as a devout Jew, ironically describing himself as 'in zeal for religion a persecutor of the church, by the law's standard of righteousness without fault' (3:6). All this he repudiated 'for the sake of gaining Christ', concluding that 'My one desire is to know Christ and the power of his resurrection, and to share his sufferings in growing conformity with his death, in hope of somehow attaining the resurrection of the dead' (3:10-11). What he means by this hope is indicated at the end of the chapter, when he asserts that Christ 'will transfigure our humble bodies, and give them a form like that of his own glorious body, by that power which enables him to make all things subject to himself' (3:21). The secret of Paul's experience is that in the suffering and dying lies the power of God and the transformation of man. Only by the Cross is eternal life mediated and made real.

In all his letters his testimony to this experience is both strongly autobiographical and pivotal to his theology. In Romans 1:16, Paul declares that he is not ashamed of the gospel, it is the power of God unto salvation; in 5:10-11 he claims that reconciliation only comes through the death of Christ on the Cross. In chapter 6, he associates the mystery of living through dying with baptism itself. In 8:17, he links suffering and glory together as the meaning of Christian experience, and in 8:31-37 he affirms that it is only in the midst of suffering that the victory of the resurrection is encountered and made real. In 12:17-21, Paul insists that 'love of enemies' alone defeats evil.

In Galatians, which is more strongly autobiographical, this note is more insistently struck. It is in 2:20 that Paul confesses that he has been 'crucified with Christ'. In 3:4, he recalls the suffering which the Galatian church experienced in consequence of conversion as a sign of the authenticity of the gospel; while in 4:13-14 he reminds them of the visible sufferings he displayed when he first came to them as an evangelist. In 4:19, he asserts that his present anxiety and suffering on their behalf are a life-giving travail 'until Christ be formed' (RV) in them; and towards the end of that chapter he indicates that conflict of a spiritual character is endemic to faith under the old covenant, and now under the new also. He is quite clear that Jews who persecute him do so because they find the gospel of the Cross a scandal (5:11); and he concludes his letter with a personal postscript (6:11-18) in which he says that the only 'glory' men can receive comes through accepting crucifixion with Christ. The result is a 'new creation'; and in his own case Paul bears in his body the 'marks' (Greek *stigmata*) of Jesus.

In 1 Thessalonians, echoes of this teaching occur frequently, though in a more circumstantial manner. In 2:2, Paul recalls how he spoke to them of the gospel of God 'in face of great opposition', refusing 'honour from men' (2:6). Suffering is the hallmark of Christianity, and the bond which draws churches together (2:14); it is also an inescapable part of the Christian vocation (3:4-5).

The way in which Paul sets out to puncture the spiritual compla-cency and pride of elements in the Corinthian church in his first letter to them is precisely to emphasise that 'the foolishness of God is wiser than men; and the weakness of God is stronger than men' (1 Cor. 1:25 RV). This is the meaning of the gospel of a crucified Messiah. Paul actually claims to embody this truth in the manner of his preaching, by which the power of the Spirit is mediated (2:1-5). With consummate irony, he debunks the worship of visible success by the leading Corinthian Christians by indicating how genuine apostles have to endure becoming 'fools' for the sake of Christ; he lists the depth of humiliation which is his lot as the only proof of his genuineness as an evangelist (4:6-13). It is an important passage. Then, in 9:26-27, Paul indicates how far removed he is from any shred of his old Pharisaic complacency: he subjects himself to ascetic discipline in order not to run the risk of missing the mark through pride at his own labours. It is in 13:4-8 that Paul expounds the meaning of Christlike love and its endurance as the only antidote to spiritual pride and power; this love is something which by its very nature points beyond itself to the reality and glory of eternal life. In 15:53-57, he is able to give startling meaning to belief in resurrection in language which speaks out of deep inner experience; and in 16:13-14 he hints at the conflict to be endured by faith in order to prevail simply by the power of love alone.

It is in the opening chapter of his letter to the Colossians that Paul places the mystery of suffering in Christ within the wider perspective of his doctrine of Christ as the means of human salvation. The Cross is the place where this occurs, and its scope is cosmic. But Paul concludes with these striking words: 'It is now my joy to suffer for you; for the sake of Christ's body, the church, I am completing what still remains for Christ to suffer in my own person' (Col. 1:24). This is an important clue to the meaning of the 'mystery' and the 'glory' of which he speaks – the gospel to be proclaimed to the Gentiles. The word which he uses to describe this 'filling up' or 'completing' of Christ's sufferings is unique here, though the conviction is echoed elsewhere in the Pauline writings (e.g. 2 Tim. 2:10; Eph. 3:13). It indicates how deep in his mind was the link between the sacrifice of Christ on the Cross, the experience and work of an apostle, and the meaning of the church's life as the Body of Christ. So, at the end of the same chapter in Colossians, Paul concludes that his own labour in the power of the Spirit is to enable people to grow to their perfection in Christ. His toil is life-giving.

All these themes, which spring from a common core of experience and belief, are taken up and developed in the most autobiographical of all his letters, 2 Corinthians. Here may be found the fullest and deepest expression of Paul's personal experience of life in union with Christ crucified and risen. Here may be seen most clearly what it meant for him to be 'in Christ'. By listening carefully to how he seeks to convey the reality, and at times the awfulness, of this experience, it is possible to enter deeply into what he meant by the pregnant words 'the glory of this mystery ... which is Christ in you, the hope of glory' (Col. 1:27 RV).

Paul's second letter to the church at Corinth arose out of further controversy between himself and sections of the church there. The connection with his earlier letter is not entirely clear, but it is unlikely that these two letters comprise the entire correspondence between Paul and the church involved. The interest and value of the second letter lie in the amount of passionate autobiographical testimony it contains to Paul's inner life and experience as a Christian evangelist. In it lies the heart of his witness and message.

The letter opens with a prayer to God which takes up and elaborates what Paul says elsewhere about suffering for the sake of the Body of Christ – the church. As in Romans 8:15, Paul describes God as 'Father' – the Father of Christ and of Christians too (2 Cor. 1:3-4). He is the 'Father of mercies' (cf. Rom. 12:1-2), the source of all the many compassionate acts recounted in the Old Testament, culminating in the gift of Christ and of the Spirit. He is also the 'God of all comfort'. As 'comforter' he is active in relationship with his children, and the verb 'to comfort' in Greek has a wide range of meaning which includes summoning, inviting assistance, urging, exhorting, appealing, encouraging and consoling: in short involving men and women in a most demanding but also a most supportive relationship.

As in Isaiah 63:9, God supports his people in all affliction: 'In all their affliction he was afflicted' (RV). For each kind of affliction there is the appropriate divine comfort: strength, relief and closeness to God. The word 'affliction' has a special range of meaning in the New Testament, derived from its basic Greek usage in the Septuagint to mean 'adverse pressure'. It speaks of external distress and of internal pain and stress, mental or spiritual. In the gospels it also has an eschatological significance; for example in John 16:21 it is associated with the 'birth-pangs' of a new age. In Colossians 1:24 (cf. RV), Paul uses the word to describe the life-giving sufferings of Christ in which Christians are called to share. In the Sermon on the Mount, Jesus declares: 'narrow is the gate and constricted [or 'afflicted'] is the road that leads to life, and those who find them are few' (Matt. 7:14). Paul is going to show the true nature of this afflicted Christian way and the eternal life to which it leads.

In the opening verses of 2 Corinthians, Paul also demonstrates the way in which the Body of Christ, the church, is an organic unity in which there is a flow of life-giving and suffering love between Christ the head and each member. It is perhaps the special vocation of the apostle or Christian leader to enter deeply in a particular way into the sufferings of Christ so that his or her own life may become life-giving also (cf. John 7:37-39). The suffering of Christ has 'no limit' in its nature; but neither has the 'consolation' it brings. Suffering shared and consolation exchanged, that is the bond of love between Christians, their common lot 'bearing one another's burdens, and so fulfilling the law of Christ' (Gal. 6:2). But this compassionate sharing is rooted in the common belief that such suffering has meaning, and will not in the end prove unendurable, because of God's presence within it. Here lies the root of that *koinonia* ('fellowship'), the hallmark of the church, which means nothing less than participation in the life-giving sufferings of Christ himself.

In the next few verses, Paul refers to actual sufferings he endured during his travels in Asia Minor (cf. Acts 19:23; and perhaps 1 Cor. 15:32). The language he employs here (1:8-11) is intended to convey directly their inner spiritual impact and significance. The 'extraordinary' nature of this onset of 'affliction' is stressed, and frequently in this letter the word 'extraordinary' or 'exceedingly' marks the initiative of divine grace. The situation he faced was overwhelmingly burdensome, oppressive beyond normal conditions, and virtually unsupportable by natural resources. Paul admits that despair set in, in words which echo Psalm 88:15 (the Septuagint text). This ancient prayer, wrung out of acute suffering, conveys the grimness of the affliction Paul was in, an experience intensely personal though also shared in part with his companions. He is now looking back at a moment which proved a spiritual turning-point: a real whiff of death itself, with a finality comparable to an execution, so that thereafter a whole of way of living, naturally self-reliant, was jettisoned. This experience of dying in the midst of life was clearly real enough for him to enter more deeply into what it means for God to raise the dead. He communicates an ultimately indescribable moment: a furnace of suffering in which trust towards God was forged in a radically new and lasting way, a moment of divine 'rescue' common in the language of the Psalms.

The passage concludes with an important affirmation about the role of intercession within the Body of Christ. This reaching out in faith and love, even by those ignorant of the solitary and dreadful plight of the apostle, is a genuine and effectual cooperation in love, a feat of spiritual solidarity. It yields a 'gift' of which Paul and those who shared his plight were the beneficiaries, which is itself both the fruit and the inspiration of sacrificial thanksgiving.

The letter passes on to deal with matters affecting Paul's relationship and communications with the Corinthian church during his recent travels, in a remarkably frank and sensitive manner and with many illuminating asides. Towards the end of chapter 2 he explains how he felt led by the Spirit to seize an evangelistic opportunity while in Troas in Asia, even though he had been frustrated in his planned rendezvous with Titus. Then he breaks into an astonishing prayer of thanksgiving to God (2:14-17). This is a highly significant passage and is stamped by many of the most idiosyncratic features of Paul's writing. It uses liturgical and sacrificial language. It tries to convey the depth of union with Christ and the perilous nature of effective evangelism. It does not shy away from the tragic reality of judgement and human self-destruction. It indicates a divine and heavenly presence at work in the midst of the most unpromising circumstances. It speaks boldly too against those who would water down the gospel to save their own skins. Finally it testifies to an immediate sense of direct personal relationship with God in Christ.

This passage arises from the recollection of a situation of adversity, perplexity and personal frustration. But it commences with a note of thanksgiving, as Paul is able to discern in all circumstances the continual process by which God accomplishes his perfect will. The pattern is clear in his own mind, even if each time that he is plunged into conflict and pain seems a veritable dying. For the note of living through dying is implicit in the language used here, which is paradoxical if precise. Paul describes God's action as leading captives in a triumphal procession as part of Christ's spoils (cf. Col 2:15 and Mark 3:27). In this way a Christian partakes of Christ's victory while still in the world. The ambiguity is both ironic and deliberate. For subjection to Christ means humiliation by the world and in its eyes; yet, at the same time, the submission of the human will in love enables God to fulfil his purpose in history and so to thwart and overcome the enemy, evil. The language deployed here is an indirect commentary on the meaning of the humiliation and crucifixion of Christ himself.

The word for 'fragrance' is very significant (cf. similar usage in Phil. 4:18 and Eph. 5:2). The word can mean an unpleasant odour as well as a pleasant fragrance, and the ambivalence is emphasised by Paul here. As the meaning of the Cross and resurrection of Christ, and their reality, are revealed in the witness of a Christian, so God's judgement appears in people's divergent response. Judgement and salvation are two aspects of one divine operation. In 2 Cor. 2:16, Paul spells this out in the words which literally mean 'a stench from death itself to the dying, and a fragrance from life itself to the living'. The tragedy of the gospel is that it is both attractive and repulsive. Therein lies the cost of the life 'in Christ'.

In Paul's experience, therefore, the awesome reality of Calvary – the judgement it constitutes as well as the victory it achieves – became present as he proceeded with his mission. He sensed and endured it in himself. It is hardly surprising if he concludes with the words: 'Who is equal to such a calling?' Early in the next chapter he will answer his own question: 'There is no question of our having sufficient power in ourselves; we cannot claim anything as our own. The power we have comes from God' (3:5). 'Sufficiency' is a key word throughout this letter as Paul tries to communicate exactly what this 'sufficiency' in Christ actually means.

He is adamant that the hallmark of genuine Christianity and effective evangelism is its sacrificial character. It was because his own ministry was sacrificial that it was joyful. For the preaching of the gospel is by its very nature the setting forth of Calvary, an essentially sacrificial proclamation which is never without cost to those called to proclaim it. The gospel message is actually embodied in the person of the evangelist, his outward example and his inner suffering. There is no escaping this, and echoing the stern words of Isaiah 1:22, Paul condemns those who would adulterate the word of God for gain, or who toy with men's lives and their ultimate salvation for self-gratification or delusion. Instead Paul defines Christian sincerity not only as purity of motive towards those to whom he is preaching, but also as immediate accountability to God: 'when we declare the word we do it in sincerity, as from God and in God's sight, as members of Christ' (2:17). The word 'fragrance', therefore, signifies a tangible and ineluctable process under way in time and place, indicated by the pattern of conscious and half-conscious choices which people make continually, a pattern which comes to a focus in response to the preaching of the gospel. Before God, and certainly before the truth about Christ crucified and risen, there is no neutral ground anywhere. There is bound to be a reaction which will in the end propel a person towards either life or death in ultimate spiritual terms.

Already Paul has laid down the parameters of Christian experience. 'Affliction' is as inescapable as the 'comfort' of God's grace and love. Compassion – both shared suffering and shared love – is the bond which sustains the church in the world as an organic fellowship of human beings sharing a common life 'in Christ'. Christian ministry and evangelism have to embrace the way of the Cross, which means being assailed by severe spiritual hostility and experiencing a genuine 'dying' repeatedly. The experience, although solitary, is also shared and supported by the prayer and love of others. The outcome of such grim encounters is a deeper love of humanity. It is a sacrificial life through which the awesome reality of Calvary is mediated to men and women. It entails public humiliation and misunderstanding, and an inner sense of failure and pain. The gospel is at once appealing and disturbing, and the cost of human reaction is borne by the disciple of the Lord. This is the narrow and afflicted way of which Jesus spoke, to which Paul was called, and whose nature he is now articulating.

Chapter Two

The way – II

*"Thus death is at work in us,
but life in you."*

Chapter 2

The way – II

In chapter 3 of 2 Corinthians, Paul launches into the great sermon which dominates the middle of his letter. He is describing the ministry of the Holy Spirit in which his own life as an apostle is caught up: 'it is he who has empowered us as ministers of a new covenant' (v. 6). The gospel constitutes the new covenant between God and man, and the existence of the church is the sign of its reality. How does the new community of the covenant stand in relation to that of the old? This was perhaps the most pressing question confronting the earliest Christians, most of whom were also devout Jews. Paul's own ministry stood at the sharp end of this issue and the conflict it caused.

This new covenant of the Spirit is life-giving (v. 6), and it is endowed with a divine glory which eclipses, while fulfilling, that which accompanied the giving of the Law to Moses on Sinai (vv. 7-9). The new covenant is freely open to all who will accept it, Jew or Gentile, and it stands in true succession to that mediated by the Law, because the purpose of the Old Testament has been fully revealed in Christ; and the Spirit who communicated the old covenant now speaks through it still in the light of Christ to the children of the new (vv. 13-16). This is consistent teaching throughout the New Testament, notably in John and Hebrews. The challenge to devout Jews is to turn to Christ and to look again at their religion and its traditions in the light provided by the Spirit. The challenge to the apostle is to 'speak out boldly' (v. 12), for the gospel of Christ is God's direct communication to man, and the work of the Spirit is to bring about that miracle of communication.

Now the Lord ... is the Spirit; and where the Spirit of the Lord is, there is liberty. And because for us there is no veil over the face, we all see as in a mirror the glory of the Lord, and we are being transformed into his likeness with ever-increasing glory, through the power of the Lord who is the Spirit. (3:17-18)

With these momentous words Paul introduces the great theme of his ensuing sermon: the movement in Christian experience from glory through darkness to light. In a brief compass he has asserted the sovereignty of the Holy Spirit over Scripture and his unique role in revealing the things of Christ (cf. John 16:13). He has indicated the reality of a transforming vision at the heart of Christianity (cf. 1 Cor. 13:12). The consequence is freedom, a word used uniquely here in this letter, but close in spirit to the saying of Jesus: 'you will know the truth, and the truth will set you free' (John 8:32).

Christians are able by looking into Scripture to see, as in a mirror, Christ himself in a direct and personal way which is open to all. It is a vision which transforms those who receive it into the likeness of Christ so that their lives reflect that which they see. It is the dynamic process at the heart of Christian faith, prayer and thought, because the change is wrought by the Holy Spirit within. Openness to God means also openness to man. In Christianity the medium and the message are one; means and ends must be consistent. True confidence in God through Christ sets a person free to relate openly and honestly with others, communicating the gospel to them in a way which reflects the way God himself respects the essential freedom of man. Hence Paul's appeal to conscience in the opening part of chapter 4 (cf. 1 Pet. 3:15-16). Deceitful manipulation of men's minds is not God's mode of conversion: love expressed by moral appeal, and reasonable persuasion in dialogue with others is the only way to win people's free and genuine response. Yet evangelism does not always prevail simply by those means, and many reject such an appeal all the time. The rejection ultimately has deeper roots in the spiritual conflict being waged over the hearts and minds of men and women. In such situations, the ministry of evangelism is often a thankless task, where it is easy to lose heart. The gospel of the Cross continually has to face up to and live with the pain of human rejection, and the implacable hostility of evil. The glory, the darkness and the light are entwined.

Their unbelieving minds are so blinded by the god of this passing age that the gospel of the glory of Christ, who is the image of God, cannot dawn upon them and bring them light. It is not ourselves that we proclaim; we proclaim Christ Jesus as Lord and ourselves as your servants for Jesus's sake. For the God who said, 'Out of darkness light shall shine,' has caused his light to shine in our hearts, the light which is knowledge of the glory of God in the face of Jesus Christ. (4:4-6)

This is a passage of fundamental importance for the whole way in which Paul understands the mystery of the gospel. He has already spoken of the divisive impact of the message of the Cross (cf. 2:15-16); now he sets forth how 'The light shines in the darkness, and the darkness has never mastered it' (John 1:5). The real possibility of human persistence in rejection of the truth is seen as a deep spiritual blindness or darkness. It is a matter of the will, and the miracle of 'illumination' which reveals the glory of Christ cannot occur where it is refused. As spokesmen for Christ, like the prophets of old, Christian evangelists face this darkness and tragedy as Christ himself did. They feel it personally, even though they are hardly promoting themselves. This travail is part of their servanthood: it is a circle they cannot square – how the miracle of seeing and believing can occur in them and others, but not in all. This anguish is apparent in every book of the New Testament.

Yet, in the mind of Paul, there is a clear line of divine consistency expressed in the miracle of creation, the miracle of Christ, and the miracle of human conversion. The glory of Christ reveals the glory of God himself, as the Transfiguration narratives in the gospels make clear. For the Christian there is indeed light in the darkness, something palpable, memorable, life-transforming and deeply spiritual in nature which opens up a new degree of vision 'from glory to glory'. Never is this more true than when facing in the Spirit and for Christ the world's darkness, rejection and unbelief. Thus in the actual proclamation of the gospel, a Christian is drawn by the glory, through the darkness, to the light of Christ himself. The gospel pattern underlying the ministry of Jesus is replicated in that of his disciples.

Paul's catalogue in chapter 4 of the afflictions which accompany the preaching of the gospel is paralleled elsewhere in his letters, and in each case the language used is very precise. For example, in 1 Corinthians 4:9-13 he lampoons the pretensions of some of the church leaders there, contrasting their spiritual pride and complacency with his own 'weakness' as a 'fool for Christ', a 'spectacle to the whole universe'. His irony is biting. (Later, in 2 Corinthians 11:22-31, he again outlines his fate as an apostle, the double cross of rejection by men and deep concern for the churches.) At the end of this sermon, in 2 Corinthians 6:3-10, he reveals why this must be so. Meanwhile the 'treasure' of which he speaks in 4:7 is of course Christ within; the Christian is a lamp of clay in which the true light shines. The fragility of human life, indwelt by the Spirit, is emphasised. So too is the 'power' of God at work through a Christian, flowing out of the vessel in its weakness. For through man, God reaches out to man, and the reaction is that which assailed the true Light when he came into the world.

The assault is relentless (4:8-9). 'Affliction' comes from all quarters, physical, mental and spiritual, yet in the midst of it all a Christian is protected from being utterly destroyed. Perplexity may obscure one's vision of faith, hope and love, and of the will of God in a situation, but it will not end in utter despair, though it may drive one very near to it. Often there will be a sense of hostility and being pursued by evil, sometimes in human form, but one is never alone even if one feels alone. Things may happen which throw a person, and strike him down physically or emotionally, by way of circumstances or relationships, or by more subtle means of spiritual opposition, but the outcome will prove in the end not to be destructive despite the clear intention of the antagonist. Elsewhere in this letter Paul admits openly to the torment which often surrounded him: 'we still found no relief; instead trouble met us at every turn, fights without and fears within' (7:5).

Further on, in 11:20 Paul rebukes the Corinthian church for being so easily led by false leaders who in fact manipulate and mistreat the flock. But the language in which he mocks them is wrung out of bitter experience of the searing impact of evil assaulting a person or group of people: 'If someone tyrannises over you, exploits you, gets you in his clutches, puts on airs, and hits you in the face, you put up with it!' This is a well-known human phenomenon, most evident in the case of a dictatorship. But its root lies in the way evil seeks to crush the human spirit and destroy the personality and all forms of human community. It was the destiny to which Christ bowed himself in humiliation and death in order to liberate mankind from the tyranny of evil. Each word used by Paul here precisely describes a deeply destructive process, a dying endured: slavery, being eaten up or consumed, deluded and trapped, patronised and pushed around, and finally treated with contempt. He is not describing a reciprocal relationship at all, but a domination whose threat he knows from his own experience.

To return to chapter 4, in verses 10-12 Paul explicitly identifies this experience of evil persecution with the crucifixion of Jesus himself:

> Wherever we go we carry with us in our body the death that Jesus died, so that in this body also the life that Jesus lives may be revealed. For Jesus's sake we are all our life being handed over to death, so that the life of Jesus may be revealed in this mortal body of ours. Thus death is at work in us, but life in you.

This emphasis on the historical person of Jesus is very striking: as in Philippians 2:5ff. and 3:10-11, the sufferings of Jesus which heralded his resurrection were the point in his life with which Paul strongly identified. He asserts that this vulnerability to suffering is a state of affairs from which there is no permanent relief in this life for the Christian. It is both irksome and burdensome – a bearing of the Cross experienced in the personal life of the body, a passive humiliation of the whole person, body, mind and spirit. It is an experience of the utter barrenness, futility and horror of spiritual death which threatens the very meaning of human life and personal existence and the value of human relationships.

Yet in all this the reality and power of the risen Jesus are being revealed and made active through a life lived in this way. This being handed over to the inroads of death is the meaning of Christian life here and now, because it is conformity to the will of God revealed supremely in Jesus on the Cross. Christ in us goes on destroying death by death in time, history and human relationships. This is his way, God's way, of bringing life out of death. The assaults of evil and death upon the life and witness of a person in Christ, though they often smack of betrayal and despair, are in fact permitted by God. For through such real human fleshly suffering and humiliation, a deep work of life-giving love is being accomplished, which constitutes the mystery of the church's existence, the source of the true power of the Spirit at work in her for the life and deliverance of mankind and the created universe.

Paul concludes with a great affirmation of faith in the whole process of living through dying. It points forward to the final consummation of God's purpose, and the eternal kingdom of the resurrection in which he and his hearers will together share (vv. 13-15). All that happens in this life is part of the divine work or grace, and its reality and power are expressed by the church in eucharistic celebration. Grace, thanksgiving and glory to God are at the heart of the church's life and experience. Paul prefaces his affirmation with words drawn from Psalm 116 (the Septuagint version), with the spirit of which he clearly identifies in this context, a spirit of faith wrought out of deep suffering to the point of death. Such psalms gave him the vocabulary for clarifying the meaning of what was happening to him in the light of Christ's sufferings and the historic sufferings of his people.

This profound and continual experience of living through dying alters in a dynamic way a Christian's attitude towards the reality of eternal life.

No wonder we do not lose heart! Though our outward humanity is in decay, yet day by day we are inwardly renewed. Our troubles are slight and short-lived, and their outcome is an eternal glory which far outweighs them, provided our eyes are fixed, not on the things that are seen but on the things that are unseen; for what is seen is transient, what is unseen is eternal. (vv. 16-18)

The insistence on the daily character of this experience is characteristic, and in 1 Corinthians 15:31 (RV) he describes it more forcefully, saying: 'I die daily'. The contrast he draws with the 'outward' man and the 'inner' man echoes the way he handles his inner spiritual conflict and turmoil in Romans 7:22. But the tension described here is more than a moral conflict of the will. It indicates a deep tension within the whole person in his bodily existence, and in the next chapter of 2 Corinthians he goes on to show how this is the beginning of the resurrection process which will finally result in eternal life. It is because of his present experience that Paul is able to speak with assurance about the nature of the resurrection in 1 Corinthians 15 and elsewhere, for example in Colossians 3:10, where the renewal of human nature is similarly asserted.

His description of affliction in 2 Corinthians 4:17 is also distinctive. He stresses its essentially transitory nature in relation to eternity, but he means by that two things: firstly, that it is pressing, inescapable but quickly dissipated; then, that it is 'light', not in the simple sense of 'easy', but rather 'quick', 'nimble', 'impetuous', 'frivolous', 'fickle', and 'vacillating'. Later fathers associate attacks of this character with the operations of demons, the perverse but deliberate assaults of evil upon the human heart, mind and will. Paul's belief is that, despite appearances and feelings at the time, behind the blows of evil lies the burnishing and transforming hand of God himself, bringing the full weight of his own glory to bear on the person whom he is refashioning after the likeness of his Son. Consequently, in and through such adversities, the sense of the eternal reality of God's love and purpose becomes more dominant, and what happens here is seen creatively in an eternal perspective (cf. Rom. 8:35-9). This is *not* an escape from present experience. Instead it is an investing of all that happens here with the divine purpose and meaning of love.

The fact that this whole process of divine remaking occurs within the bodily and personal experience of a Christian therefore invests that life with its unique significance. The opening verses of chapter 5 express this belief, concluding with the words: 'It is for this destiny that God himself has been shaping us; and as a pledge of it he has given us the Spirit' (v. 5). This remaking of man constitutes his real justification before God, delivering him from exposure to divine judgement, but at the same time making every action and attitude of bodily life accountable before God in ultimate moral and personal terms (cf. 1 Cor. 6:19-20). So although the tension often experienced induces a profound longing to be 'at home with the Lord' (cf. Phil.

1:21-4), this sense of a heavenly destiny and of divine involvement and purpose in all that happens enables faith to produce a bold and hopeful approach to life in this world. But the presence of the Spirit within, and the imposition upon daily life that this process of divine remaking represents, cause the tension in Christian living to be expressed in profound prayer, the 'yearning' or 'groaning' which, as Paul shows in Romans 8:23 and 26, is the intercession of the Holy Spirit himself in man. So Christian bodily life more and more straddles the boundary between time and eternity as a person's life is drawn closer into the orbit of God's life and love. Paul concludes by asserting the inescapable and complete nature of divine judgement before which every human action 'in the body' stands exposed (v. 10). This principle of accountability, which underlies all Christian ethics, an accountability in love towards both God and man, also underlies Paul's understanding of evangelism, and the way Christ reaches out to mankind in its great need. For evangelism is impelled by an overwhelming sense both of God's love and of his judgement.

Paul has now established the relationship between the church of the new covenant and the religion of the old. Christ is the key to the Old Testament; Christians are heirs to the promises to Israel; the same Spirit speaks and illuminates the Scriptures. The glory of God in the face of Christ transforms those who behold it in their relationship to God and to their fellow-men. They come to embody him whom they proclaim, and to experience the same mixed human response, including the pain of rejection. The glory reveals the darkness in man, a darkness which assails the Christian evangelist. Paul draws on his own personal experience to indicate quite precisely the nature and pattern of 'affliction' which is the Christian's lot. He has no illusions about the operations of evil or their destructive intent towards the human spirit and personality (cf. Eph. 6:10f). But this suffering he sees as a participation in the suffering of the crucified Jesus, the means by which God renews human nature, and transforms it, while in time and space, into resurrection and eternal life. All that happens in Christian life is thus invested with a supreme meaning whose fulfilment lies beyond in the eternal kingdom of God's life and love. Christian bodily life is being drawn painfully but truly into the existence of heaven itself: both prayer and evangelism spring from this experience and process.

Chapter Three

The way – III

"The love of Christ controls us."

Chapter 3

The way – III

All that Paul says in the remainder of his great sermon (2 Cor. 5:11-6:10) about the nature of evangelism springs from his own experience of living through dying, and the changes in perception which that brings. The apostle preaches with a sense of the immediate presence of God, in the 'fear of the Lord'. Like his Lord he can only persuade, he cannot compel. He lays his conscience open to the criticism of his fellow-Christians – a common note in the New Testament. It is simple integrity and openness pitted against subtle hypocrisy and self-assertion (v. 12). This is the inevitable result of a life lived between heaven and earth: 'For whether we are beside ourselves, it is unto God; or whether we are of sober mind, it is unto you' (v. 13 RV). The word 'to be out of one's mind' may be ironic, or it may refer to a particular episode in the past shared with the Corinthians. More likely, it testifies to Paul's contemplative and mystical spiritual experience as he 'faced' God in prayer, overawed by direct apprehension of the divine presence. But if so this is not something with which to bamboozle the Corinthians (cf. 1 Cor. 14:18-19); instead it enables him to relate to them with complete integrity, a word used to indicate sanity, chastity, and deliverance from passion. As in the life of Jesus, ministry proceeds from prayer, from a right relationship with God.

> For the love of Christ controls us once we have reached the conclusion that one man died for all and therefore all mankind has died. He died for all so that those who live should cease to live for themselves, and should live for him who for their sake died and was raised to life. (vv. 14-15)

The range of meaning comprehended in the terse sentence, 'the love of Christ controls [or 'constrains', cf. Acts 18:5] us', is vast, and pregnant with great significance. The verb can mean 'to sustain', 'to foreclose upon and hem in, actually to hold in custody to the point of distress', 'to absorb' and 'to impel', 'to control', and even 'to include or embrace'. Each of these meanings indicates a way in which the 'love of Christ', both our love for him and his for us, bears upon Christian life. 'To put love in where love is not' (St John of the Cross) is the meaning of the Incarnation, supremely revealed upon Calvary; it is also the meaning of the church and its mission, here embodied in the person and activity of the apostle and evangelist. Thus evangelism springs out of living through dying, of being caught up in the love and will of Christ. For without Christ, men and women are a slowly dying breed, trapped by sin and evil. But by his death the sheer inevitability of this destructive death is reversed; and by accepting a dying to self in Christ, a new life can begin even in the midst of this dying world. All mankind stands in a relationship to Christ, either to judgement or to life. The death of Jesus has therefore a universal and a personal significance (cf. Rom. 5:15). All human life is now seen from the height of Calvary.

The destiny of man therefore lies in the possibility and reality of resurrection. The evangelist no longer judges people from a merely human point of view, but from this divine perspective. Even the meaning of the Messiahship of Jesus only becomes fully clear in the light of his death and resurrection (v. 16). So Paul can assert: 'For anyone united to Christ, there is a new creation; the old order has gone; a new order has already begun' (v. 17; cf. Rom. 6:4; Gal. 6:15). This is the heart of the matter. The new is born in the midst of and by the dying of the old, just as the seed springs to new life out of the husk of what was buried (cf. 1 Cor. 15:42ff.; John 12:24). The conscious experience of this process of living through dying is the essence of Christianity, of the life 'in Christ'.

'All this has been the work of God. He has reconciled us to himself through Christ, and has enlisted us in this ministry of reconciliation' (v. 18). So the great teaching about the atonement set forth in Romans is now applied to the heart of evangelism. Through the mission of the church, through the apostles and evangelists, God reaches out to man through man; and as verse 19 hints, the scope of this divine work of reconciliation is cosmic (cf. Col. 1:20). The Christian is God's 'ambassador'; sometimes, as in Ephesians 6:20, an ambassador 'in chains'. An ambassador is a representative and spokesman, also a presence and an embodiment of the values of the kingdom he represents. So the word describing God's 'appeal' to mankind through the life and witness of the church speaks of invitation, encouragement, persuasion, conciliation and comfort (v. 20). Evangelism and pastoral relationship stand together in a bond of humility and love towards those to whom God's invitation is being extended. Only thus can the solemn message of the Cross be proclaimed: 'Christ was innocent of sin, and yet for our sake God made him one with human sinfulness, so that in him we might be made one with the righteousness of God' (v. 21).

Christians are fellow-workers with the Holy Spirit in God's great mission to the world in Christ (6:1), and Paul is quick to appeal directly to his hearers in the Corinthian church lest they miss their vocation. Commenting upon a reference to Isaiah 49:68 in verse 2, he insists upon the immediate and eschatological urgency of this mission of evangelism: 'This is the hour of favour, this the day of deliverance'. Christians too must respond afresh to the message of the Cross, lest they empty the gospel of its meaning and life-giving power in their own lives. Probably once again this citation of a small part of a famous passage in Isaiah is a pointer to the wider ambit of what Paul had in mind. For Isaiah 49 is likely to have been a scripture which Paul took very much to heart in a personal way as an evangelist. It describes the Servant of the Lord as one predestined by God, one who embodies the true destiny of Israel. This destiny includes an outreach to the Gentiles: 'I shall appoint you a light to the nations, so that my salvation may reach to earth's farthest bounds' (Isa. 49:6). In Romans 15:16ff. Paul describes his mission very much in these terms. Although despised and rejected by men, this Servant will be rescued and protected in order to gather together the scattered people of God, Jews and Gentiles alike, so restoring the covenant and placing it upon a cosmic foundation, 'for the Lord has comforted his people, and has had pity on them in their distress' (Isa. 49:13). The language of Paul's gloss on the verse from Isaiah which he cites is both eschatological and liturgical, words which echo the gospels as they indicate a total personal response to God's grace which is at once deeply sacrificial and immediate.

Paul concludes his great sermon by indicating exactly what this sacrificial self-offering means in terms of how evangelism is conducted and what it costs. It is a personal testimony, but it could also be taken as an indirect commentary upon the ministry of Jesus himself, who 'son though he was ... learned obedience through his sufferings' (Heb. 5:8).

Paul is insistent in 6:3-10 that the Christian must not lay himself open to any justifiable censure by others; there must be no tangible grounds for scandal. For the message of the gospel will give offence to many, but the life of the person presenting it must not, lest that be made an excuse for its rejection. Ministry, which is God's own ministry of reconciliation, cannot rest on hypocrisy. Instead, in every kind of circumstance, fair or foul, it is God's ministry in Christ that his servants are commending: what are its hallmarks? Although expressed in terms of personal experience in relation to external persecutions, this careful catalogue sets forth the inner spiritual conflict and nature of Christian life lived within the Body of Christ, the church. These are the hallmarks of the church's life and witness because they are the pattern of how Christ himself related to the world he came to save.

The foundation of Christian living is patience and 'steadfast endurance' (v. 4), biding God's time to see his glory; and this entails fortitude, perseverance, constancy and a lively expectation of God's purpose already at work in a situation, despite appearances. A Christian is assailed by afflictions, external and internal, which take the form of calamities, trials and temptations which cannot be avoided. Life feels crushed under the anguish of distress, narrowed down, hemmed in and besieged. Misfortunes strike real and deep blows, sometimes in physical form, never without mental and spiritual torment. Such imprisonment of spirit can be actual or psychological, more than a whiff of hell itself. Yet a Christian must 'stand in hell, and despair not' (St Silouan of Mount Athos). The word for 'mobbed' (v. 5) describes a state of insurrection prompted by evil, profound disturbance and upheaval which threaten a person's sense of inner security and identity; it suggests an implacable spiritual opposition. In such circumstances the ministry of the gospel seems difficult, dangerous, and troublesome, a real hardship and toil, a labour of love without any immediate sign of reward or success. It becomes an imposition upon personal life and privacy, with sleepless nights of care, watching and prayer, aggravated by hardships and afflictions, while all the time one is hungering and thirsting for peace, security and happiness, as well as for God himself.

This is a veritable dying. But the consequences of this ascetic way are divine attributes and characteristics brought to birth within the life and ministry of the Christian. For evangelism and sanctity are closely conjoined, and both have their root in living through dying. From this crucible of divine love proceed purity and sincerity, genuine knowledge and understanding of divine truth, long-suffering, steadfast endurance in relationships towards other people, the patience of God himself. Similarly goodness, kindness and generosity, those 'fruits' of the Spirit (cf. Gal. 5:22-23) which are the 'gifts' of a Christlike life which emulates in all things the heart of the heavenly Father himself (cf. Matt. 5:43-48). It is a life permeated by the presence of the Holy Spirit within, which results in a spirit of holiness which directly affects others, and which embodies what is being proclaimed by word and deed, because it is a life of divine love, self-giving, self-sacrificing and forgiving. This is 'life in all its fullness' (cf. John 10:10), at once deeply human and deeply divine, and life-giving to others.

It is, however, love in conflict, and the Christian therefore encounters contrary responses within the church and outside it. One set of responses springs from God and comes from those attracted to him in a genuine way. The other set expresses human rejection of the light of God's judgement and love (cf. John 3:18-21). The catalogue Paul sets forth in verses 8-10 is very carefully and perceptively balanced, being a many-sided description of reality as experienced to varying degrees by Christians. It is to be seen as a whole as well as individually, deriving its ultimate meaning from the life and death of Jesus himself. There is a price to be paid for Christian sanctity and evangelism. Human rejection and the machinations of evil pour scorn and disparagement upon Christian witness, seeking out of envy and hatred to accuse, patronise or ignore. Yet only as love of reputation is abandoned is divine glory experienced, and as the shame of the Cross is accepted so discipleship and sonship are affirmed by God. The truth of Christianity is tested by insinuations and lies, the scourge of false accusations; as Christians are isolated and rejected by their fellow-men, so they are driven closer to God himself. The world does not love those not its own, indeed it cannot (cf. John 15:18-21); and the terms Paul uses here to caricature what is said about him are not without irony.

At the heart of the ferment, Paul discerns the hidden pattern to all Christian living: 'dying we still live on; disciplined by suffering, we are not done to death'. Everything that occurs is held in the wounded hand of God himself. Thus the mystery of which Christ speaks in the beatitudes (Matt. 5) is revealed: out of sorrow joy is born, and genuine poverty before God opens the floodgates of divine blessing in us and through us. Pride and self-gratification, the two primordial sins of man, are thus overcome, and as possessiveness is abandoned so that which is of eternal value is obtained. In the words of Jesus himself: 'unless a grain of wheat falls into the ground and dies, it remains that and nothing more; but if it dies, it bears a rich harvest' (John 12:24). Sanctity and effective evangelism are part of that harvest. For as Paul affirms later in this letter: 'You know the generosity of our Lord Jesus Christ: he was rich, yet for your sake he became poor, so that through his poverty you might become rich' (8:9).

In chapters 10 and 11, Paul returns to the theme of the spiritual conflict in which he finds himself engaged so relentlessly, and to one form of it which he clearly found very irksome, namely opposition from false brethren who maligned his labours and distracted his hearers. This is a recurrent theme in his letters: it is an area of difficulty that he found hard to handle, and often his most biting irony is reserved for these antagonists. Because he consciously eschewed any attempt to persuade his hearers by human rhetoric or force of personality Paul was open to criticism and ridicule (cf. 1 Cor. 2). Here he firmly relates his demeanour as an evangelist to the example of the Lord himself who was gentle and gracious (10:1). Although he obviously found such criticism and machination personally wounding, Paul's anxiety over the impact of such false dealing by those who claim to be something which they are not lies deeper than just personal grievance. He discerns that behind their operations and insinuations lurks the malevolence of evil itself, exploiting men's needs, hurts, vulnerabilities and weaknesses, and always seeking thus to undermine and divide the church. Paul has no illusions here (10:3-6) or elsewhere (cf. Eph. 6:10ff.; 1 Thess. 5:8; 1 Tim. 1:18) about the nature and reality of the spiritual opposition which besets him at every turn, and the note of warfare is seldom absent from his writings.

Paul regarded Christ's victory on the Cross as having cosmic scope, and this is most fully expressed in Colossians 2:15, where he asserts that 'There [Christ] disarmed the cosmic powers and authorities and made a public spectacle of them, leading them in his triumphal procession'. He believed that a Christian has to enter into the sufferings of Christ because, in time and history, conflict with evil remains endemic, and is the cause of those sufferings. In Ephesians 6:10ff. he outlines explicitly the spiritual strategy required. Paul clearly reckoned with the active operations of evil, and in the life of the church he was specially exercised by the way in which the truth of the gospel could be so easily perverted (cf. 11:4), and false leaders could arise who actually treat the people of God in a shameful and tyrannical manner (11:19-20). Deception and pride are the hallmarks of the devil, and the consequence is division within the life of the church and the blunting of its witness. To challenge these pretensions for what they are, he insists on rooting the gospel and effective evangelism in the humiliating reality of suffering, and he concludes chapter 11 with an important and characteristic outline of what had happened to him in his own life and ministry. He lambasts 'sham apostles, confidence tricksters masquerading as apostles of Christ' (11:13). But as the Lord said, 'by their fruits ye shall know them' (Matt. 7:20 RV).

Paul clearly rated 'dangers from false Christians' (11:26) as a major and perennial hazard to his own ministry. The pain of the situation wore him down, as so often he felt powerless to contend with undermining influences at such a distance. The whole tenor of this letter reflects his agony, as also does 1 Corinthians. The words with which he concludes his autobiographical testimony in 11:28-31 are harrowing and wrung from the heart:

Apart from all these external things, there is the responsibility that weighs on me every day, my anxious concern for all the churches. Is anyone weak? I share his weakness. If anyone brings about the downfall of another, does my heart not burn with anger? If boasting there must be, I will boast of the things that show up my weakness.

He is never closer to the suffering of Jesus himself in his ministry than in having to contend with the permanent possibility of betrayal and falsehood, even among so-called friends and brethren. This was his personal cross. The dominant note on which Paul concludes this letter to the Corinthians is summed up in the way he insists that 'If I must needs glory, I will glory of the things that concern my weakness' (11:30 RV). This juxtaposition of 'glory' and 'weakness' is both ironic and idiosyncratic. It is ironic because it debunks the pretensions of human self-glorying, idiosyncratic because it enshrines the innermost heart of Paul's own experience as an apostle.

Chapter 12 begins with a mysterious reference by Paul to his own mystical experience as a man of deeply contemplative prayer, and its full significance as such will be discussed later. But the main reason why he adduces such testimony is to set the context for his confiding that suffering and vision in Christianity go together. At this point he overturns the aspirations of human spiritual traditions of whatever kind which claim to offer spiritual release from the world of flesh and blood and suffering in which human life is set. The full force of his remarkable testimony in 12:7-10 needs to be weighed carefully.

This experience is God's remedy to the primordial sins of pride and self-gratification which lurk deep at the heart of all human life and religion. The 'thorn in the flesh' means some grievous and inescapable imposition by evil upon Paul's personal life, which caused him spiritual, mental and at times physical pain, anguish and humiliation. It was his cross, and the word for 'thorn' is actually used as a metaphor for crucifixion in contexts outside the New Testament. Glory, darkness, light: here the gospel pattern is at its most concentrated. The place of vision is the place of suffering, and the place of suffering becomes the place where the presence of Christ himself is felt most fully. The Cross is not assumed for a while then laid aside; it is borne daily, as Jesus indicated, but in the strength of the Lord himself. Only in this way is the life of the resurrection mediated through the suffering of the saint to the church, and through the church to the world.

So Paul is aware of the presence of evil tormenting and abusing him, and at the same time of Christ who sustains him, perfecting his grace and power through his abject weakness and humiliation, and the loneliness of his sufferings. He is indeed being 'crucified with Christ', but he is 'overshadowed' by the glory and the power of the risen Lord. For the place of dying is the place of the resurrection also, where the sin of man is unmade and evil overcome. All the afflictions he lists in verse 10 are for the sake of Christ, and actually Christlike. From this 'patience' springs the miraculous renewal of man which is the hallmark of genuine, Christlike, apostolic ministry (cf. v. 12).

This divine compassion into which Paul was being drawn colours his whole relationship with the church to which he was writing. His own compassion for them is clearly evident in his closing lines, and even when he threatens the corruption that is in their midst, the authority he wields is that of humiliation and grief at that which mars the life of the Body of Christ (v. 21). In 13:3-4, 8 is found the heart of Paul's relationship with the church: Paul's life and ministry are life-giving because they embody the truth of the crucified Jesus; his is a serving authority following the example of Christ the Shepherd and Servant. His powerlessness towards his erring hearers is the relative powerlessness of God, who chooses only to persuade the unruly wills and affections of sinful men and women; for in the words of the *Epistle to Diognetus*, 'force is no attribute of God'. Christian authority is in the end something given away and given up at great cost to set others free: it is 'authority ... for building up and not for pulling down' (v. 10).

There is no coercion of men at Calvary by God, only the coercion of cruelty borne by God in man in the person of the crucified Christ. This reveals and redeems the weakness of man, and exposes and absorbs the ruthlessness of evil seeking to destroy both man and God. Calvary is the place where two wills clash, two powers are engaged, two notions of authority are displayed. Evil is swallowed up by that human nature which bears God. Into that God-bearing human nature of Christ, Christians are incorporated by baptism and faith, and are sustained in it by prayer and sacraments. St Paul was the first fully to articulate what this being 'in Christ' actually meant: the deep personal cost of Christlike suffering, and the reality of resurrection life making all things new. What he saw in himself, he saw also in the church, which he described as the Body of Christ, a body at once crucified and risen, with the power and reality of Calvary at the heart of its life: this frail humanity, through which God continues to reach out to mankind by the power of the Holy Spirit in time and history.

Chapter Four

Finding the way

"Near the sword means near to God."

Chapter 4

Finding the way

The problem of suffering is central to the Bible, and in first-century Judaism there was a well-established tradition of martyrdom for the sake of faithful obedience to the Torah, the Law. Echoes of this may be detected in the gospels quite clearly, and the murders of both John the Baptist and of Jesus himself were seen in this light. The way in which Christ retells the parable of the vineyard (Mark 12:1-12) turns an ancient prophetic oracle against the corrupt rulers of Jerusalem (cf. Isa. 5:1-7) into a stark prediction of his own impending rejection and destruction. But this event is set against the background of a long succession of maltreated prophets (cf. Heb. 11). In Luke 11:37f., in his diatribe against various elements of the religious establishment, Jesus condemns the hypocrisy of those who now venerate the martyrs whom their predecessors killed; he mounts a similar challenge in John 8:37f., accusing his antagonists of evil intentions towards him. The perennial conflict between God and evil, played out in the hearts and minds of men, runs from the murder of Abel to the present day, as Jesus also makes clear in the story of the prodigal son in Luke 15. In that story it is the suffering as a result of sin which leads to life-giving repentance, something which the elder brother, in his envy and complacency, can never experience or accept. The conflict is thus deeply entwined in Israel's history, as St Paul indicates in Galatians 4:21ff., where the strife between the offspring of Sarah and Hagar is construed as a struggle between spiritual freedom and slavery. For the writer of the fourth gospel, the great truth about the uplifting of the Son of Man on the Cross is that by it evil is thrown down and human life liberated: darkness cannot quench the divine light incarnate in Jesus. Yet the darkness which is deepest is the blindness of those who claim to see, but who reject Jesus (John 9:41). It is against this darkness which can kill others in the name and service of God (cf. John 16:2) that Stephen speaks out during his trial in Acts 7, and to it he fell victim.

The gospels and Acts confirm the testimony of St Paul that the fate of Jesus induced a profound trauma within the Jewish religion. The writers of all these texts were devout Jews who were also followers of a crucified and risen Messiah. The double tradition in Jewish religious history of perfidy and suffering had in the destruction of Jesus boiled up and over, calling into question the whole way in which that history and faith of Israel were now to be interpreted. However, the word the Christians used for the 'betrayal' of Jesus also meant his being 'delivered up' according to the will of God. The mystery of the New Testament lies in the way the pain, the conflict, the darkness and the judgement are balanced by the calm insistence on the necessity of this road of suffering for the Messiah, and its intelligibility within the long history of Israel's own suffering. Without this tradition, the deepest disclosure of God's purpose for the salvation of mankind through the heart-rending suffering of faithful Jews, culminating in the person of Jesus, could never have been revealed. In their reactions towards Jesus, for and against him, the whole drama of man before God is played out with peculiar intensity. The particularity of the Cross, and the crisis within the Jewish religion which it caused, reveal the universal dilemma and destiny of suffering mankind.

Behind the way in which these earliest Jewish Christians expressed their faith in a crucified and risen Messiah lay certain passages of the Old Testament which now took on a totally new meaning in the light of Jesus. The Cross became the key to the Old Testament, and the earliest forms of Christian exegesis tried to discern the fundamental pattern of divine activity embedded in the text of the Scriptures. Notable early examples of this tendency occur in the letters of St Paul, for example in Galatians 4:21ff. and 1 Corinthians 10:1-13. The same standpoint is axiomatic for the whole elaborate theology of Hebrews, and it is evident also in the profound metamorphosis of Jewish apocalyptic mysticism which created Revelation. The insistent note *dei pathein*, having to suffer in order to experience eternal life, is constant throughout the New Testament.

Clearly, Isaiah 53 and adjacent passages assumed a crucial role in articulating the earliest proclamations of the crucified Messiah, as the primitive tradition of sermons preached by the apostles in Acts makes clear. Almost certainly this was a distinctive hallmark of the Lord's own teaching; his insistence on being the Servant called to suffer is recorded in all the gospels (cf. Mark 10:45; John 13). The message of Acts is corroborated in 1 Peter also. Jesus is identified as God's holy 'servant' (or 'child'), glorified by him despite human rejection, a symbol of salvation anointed by God to be the source of healing for mankind.

Close reading of Isaiah 53, especially in the Greek of the Septuagint, is very striking in the light of the Cross, and from this passage sprang much of the distinctive language by which the mystery of that event was expressed by the first Christians. There is an unusual juxtaposition of imagery and language here, which subsequently came to life in the minds of those who had known Jesus and who were the witnesses to his death and resurrection. There is glory and exaltation and a claim to a universal significance. Yet there is also obscurity, rejection and ostracism of one not obviously attractive or intelligible to those claiming to seek him. Suffering and identification with sickness were his hallmarks, alike in life as in death. The Servant of the Lord is at once the innocent victim, the sin-offering, and the sin-bearer. Behind the apparent loneliness of his position among his own people lies a deep and costly compassion for them, but his very suffering and inner anguish mark him out for condemnation and misjudgement. In and through this affliction a complete and liberating sacrifice for human sin and wickedness is being accomplished. The sign that this is so, that this is in fact the work of God, is the silence of the victim: this is the pinnacle of his faithfulness and the final depth of his own personal humiliation. The circumstances of his death and burial prove deeply compromising and disastrous. Yet in the midst of all this there is a remarkable transition. God's continuing purpose for his Servant continues through his death, which proves to be life-giving. Still he bears the sins of his own people, but now from a position of deep understanding of the divine will, standing within that will, having been 'shown light' by the Lord in the darkness of despair and death. His death is therefore a victory; by it divine strength is revealed which will lay low all other powers. It is an extraordinary passage, pregnant with illumination for a Christian pondering the meaning of the Cross in any generation.

Another passage in the Old Testament which articulates the peculiar intensity of an apparently innocent suffering, none the less somehow related to the sins of the people and to the divine will, may be found in the Lamentations of Jeremiah. In these haunting words the city of Jerusalem in her plight, having fallen a prey to her enemies, is personified in the sufferer. There is in St Luke's gospel a strong tradition which indicates that Jesus saw his own rejection and fate in Jerusalem as prophetic of the ultimate destruction of the city by the Romans. For deep in the image of the Suffering Servant lies the truth that it is only as the Servant identifies with and is identified with the shame and the sorrow of God's people that his sacrifice is complete. In him is personified both the vocation of that people in utter faithfulness to the divine will, and the abject failure of God's people, trapped by evil in sin and anguish. For early Jewish Christians, people, city and temple all converge on the one figure of the Suffering Servant, Jesus, in whom divine judgement and divine salvation are focused and revealed. This vision underlies the theological structure of each of the gospels, in different ways.

The opening part of Lamentations is an eloquent intercession and dirge for the punishment and affliction being experienced by the Lord's people, and by the city of Jerusalem in particular. Later generations of Christian spiritual teachers found in the third chapter a potent expression of the meaning of the Cross, and of that experience of living through dying which lies at the heart of Christian ascetic prayer. They are terrible words which peer right into the darkness of Calvary itself. It is not hard to see how the experiences described by St Paul in 2 Corinthians and elsewhere, and the careful memory of the passion of Christ, found in such language a heartfelt and accurate expression.

In Lamentations 3, the writer wrestles with the meaning of life, seeking hope in the constancy of God and the fleeting nature of suffering. In the heart of this darkness there is an astonishing testimony to faith in God. Driven into the darkness of suffering, a person is brought closer to God in his innermost nature than could otherwise be the case. In the midst of human tyranny and injustice, hope reaches out towards the justice of God. Meanwhile, the sufferer goes out of himself in profound compassion for the sufferings of his people with whom he identifies. Yet, for all this the persecution grows deeper and stronger, evil pressing in through the antagonisms and betrayals of men. In the face of certain and humiliating death, God's rescue comes, and thus the passage concludes with a glimmer of hope in an ultimate vindication, of a divine action snatching a person from the jaws of destruction.

This movement from darkness to light, through suffering to salvation, by the bitter road of human rejection and isolation, prey to the assaults of evil, took on new meaning in the light of the resurrection. Embedded in these ancient testimonies and prayers could now be detected the authentic way in which God brought salvation to those faithful to him. The way, and the certainty of that way, were now opened up and confirmed in Christ's own passage through suffering from death to life.

Nowhere is this profound movement from death to life more evident than in Psalm 22, the prayer which was on the lips of Jesus as he died. These words express the agony of the Servant of God being tormented by his enemies, feeling abandoned by God and cut off from the saving history of his people. He is exposed to ridicule and made an object of contempt. His trust in God and all that he stands for is bitterly mocked. The memory of his mother's love and spiritual nurture now seems to count for nothing, while life itself ebbs away from a body wracked by pain and thirst. Powerless and naked, he watches while even his personal effects are tossed for and carried away. Desperate for God's help, he stares death in the face. That is the first half of the psalm, and it is not difficult to see how remarkably it describes what actually happened to Jesus on the Cross. But the psalm does not end there. It ends on a note of victory, in hope of vindication and of a revelation of divine power: there is to be a future, defiant of death itself. Seen in the light of Easter, Psalm 22 (like Psalm 69 also) is a psalm about crucifixion *and* resurrection.

Careful review of the psalms reveals that almost half of them can be interpreted to varying extents in this way; and their language, especially in the Greek of the Septuagint, exercised an incalculable influence on the language of Christian theology and prayer from the beginning. Examples used by St Paul have already been discussed, and it is possible and fruitful to study in the case of each psalm cited in the New Testament, the relationship between the theology being expounded and the wider context of the whole psalm, from which the precise reference being used is drawn. Common to all these psalms which are capable of being interpreted in the light of the Cross and resurrection of Jesus are a number of themes: a relentless conflict with evil; astonishing frankness about the impact of undeserved suffering; the fear of guilt and shame; and the welling up of bitter feelings of hostility towards enemies. But in the midst of deep personal suffering, humiliation and mental anguish are present divine comfort, and a sense that this suffering is caught up with the sins and judgement, and also the redemption, of God's people. It is a real encounter with death and darkness of soul, but there is expectation even there of a divine deliverance, and an insistent and obstinate hope in God's salvation, life and light, even in the midst of the deepest travail and sorrow.

The psalms provided the earliest Christians, as they had Jesus himself, with the language to express all that they experienced in themselves, both individually and corporately, as they traversed, persecuted, by the way of the Cross, the abyss of darkness and evil, and so passed from death to life, from darkness to light. What had been a dogged hope among their Jewish ancestors and contemporaries, for whom belief in resurrection was by no means a certainty, now became a living experience and reality, as they encountered in prayer and worship the crucified and risen Christ midway along the narrow and afflicted path to eternal life, the way of living through dying. Thus throughout Christian history the psalms have constituted the heart of Christian ascetic prayer and experience, being the prayer of the Lord himself and of his church, the common bond between the old Israel and the new.

Clear examples of this process of appropriating Old Testament language to account for the Christian experience of living through suffering and dying may be discerned in the writings remaining from the apostolic fathers and the earliest martyrs. The influence of St Paul is also very apparent.

The central theme, for example, of the first letter of St Clement (written c. AD 96) is how 'lowliness of mind' constitutes the true following of Christ, being itself a mirror of and a participation in the great strategy of divine patience. He is addressing conflict in the church at Corinth, the consequence of envy. This conflict is the curse of mankind from the murder of Abel to the betrayal of Peter and Paul in Rome during Nero's persecution. The lowliness of Christ is the only antidote to the pride and jealousy ruining mankind. To demonstrate this truth, he turns to Isaiah 53, prefacing his citation with these words:

> For Christ is with those who are humble, not with those who exalt themselves over his flock. The majestic sceptre of God, our Lord Jesus Christ, did not come with the pomp of arrogance or pride (though he could have done so), but in humility, just as the Holy Spirit spoke concerning him. (16)

The pattern described by the prophet and lived out by Christ, the Suffering Servant, is the key to Christian living, as Clement indicates by reference to the great patriarchs and prophets of the Bible. Finally he bids his hearers look from them to God himself: 'Let us look with the eyes of the soul on his patient will. Let us note how free from anger he is towards all his creation' (19). For the work of salvation in Christ expresses the will of God in creation also. So he urges reconciliation within the church, preferring if need be self-sacrifice and self-effacement, and heartfelt intercession for those alienated by pride and jealousy, 'so that forbearance and humility may be given them, so that they may submit, not to us but to the will of God' (56).

Clement, in common with the writers of the gospel passion narratives, lays great emphasis upon the non-resistance of Christ towards the violence and tyranny of the world's authorities. This remained the stance of the church towards all persecution, whether by the Jews or by the Roman authorities, for over three centuries. Yet as the earliest accounts of Christian martyrdom reveal, it was as the church faced the world's darkness and the virulent hostility of evil working through its persecutors, that by living through the suffering and dying it experienced also the nearness of Christ and the reality of his risen life and power. So the records of how the early Christian martyrs faced suffering and death are not only a powerful defence of human rights and liberty of individual conscience. They are also a window into the almost indescribable experience, intimated first by St Paul, of how the place of Christlike suffering – even crucifixion for the sake of Christ – became the source of eternal life and glory, both for the martyrs and for the churches of which they were members.

Nowhere is the anticipation and understanding of this more eloquently, movingly and fully articulated than in the letters of St Ignatius, Bishop of Antioch, written while he was under arrest and on his way to Rome, where he eventually died around the year AD 107. In so many ways he assumes and deepens the testimony of St Paul that the place of suffering is the place of vision, and where life is lost there life is in fact restored. The Cross, and Christian participation in its redemptive suffering, lie at the heart of all Ignatius' writings. He makes explicit what the writer of the first letter of St John leaves implicit: that it is at the Cross that the union between God and man in Jesus is most fully revealed. The movement, as in the fourth gospel itself, is from glory through darkness to light.

To the Ephesian church he writes that the church is predestined by God to an eternal glory, while being 'united and elect through genuine suffering'. In this way Christians become 'imitators of God' himself. The coming of Christ, his suffering on the Cross and the virginity of Mary are hidden mysteries, 'to be loudly proclaimed, yet which were accomplished in the silence of God'. In the darkness surrounding Calvary of which St Mark speaks, 'the abolition of death was being carried out' by God in man for man (19). God's purpose is to create a new humanity in 'the new man, Jesus Christ, involving faith in him and love for him, his suffering and resurrection'. The eucharist is the sign and pledge of this possibility, 'the medicine of immortality, the antidote we take in order not to die but to live forever in Jesus Christ' (20). In his letter to the Magnesian church he makes the same point: the life of Christ is not in us 'unless we voluntarily choose to die into his suffering' (5). In his letter to the church at Tralles, he asserts the reality of Christ's sufferings in history by reference to Christian suffering. Echoing St Paul's metaphor of the Body of Christ, Ignatius declares that suffering Christians are 'branches of the Cross, their fruit imperishable – the same Cross by which he, through his sufferings, calls you who are his members. The head, therefore, cannot be born without members, since God promises unity, which he himself is' (11). The bond of union between Christians and Christ, and between Christians themselves, lies in the suffering, life-giving love common to each and to all. From this conviction his whole theology of the ministry and unity of the church springs.

Ignatius' theology of suffering and martyrdom is most fully expressed in his letters to the churches at Smyrna and in Rome itself. The reality of the Lord's sufferings are the guarantee of the reality of Christian salvation: 'Near the sword means near to God; with the beasts means with God' (*Smyr.* 4). Because he feared that the Roman church might prevent his martyrdom, his letter to them takes on a peculiar intensity and reveals the heart of his feelings and thoughts. The language he uses might seem almost masochistic and bizarre in its force, were it not straining to proclaim his conviction that only as a person in Christ advances fully and freely to embrace the sadistic evil about to be perpetrated upon him by his fellow-men, at the behest of evil, can redemption occur. Only thus can a Christian enter fully into the mystery of Christ which was revealed once for all at Calvary. Evil cannot be ignored or bypassed; it must be encountered head-on. Suffering cannot be evaded; it must be borne – in Christ and by his strength alone. With Christ in hell, hell is overcome: the place of martyrdom is the place on earth where this victory is revealed anew and made real. Ignatius anticipates this likely event as the climax and true meaning of his own priestly ministry and vocation:

> Christianity is greatest when it is hated by the world .... Allow me to be an imitator of the suffering of my God'.... My passionate love has been crucified and there is no fire of material longing within me, but only water living and speaking in me, saying within me, "Come to the Father". I take no pleasure in corruptible food or the pleasures of this life. I want the bread of God, which is the flesh of Christ who is of the seed of David; and for drink I want his blood, which is incorruptible love. (3, 6, 7)

It seems that for Ignatius his profound devotion to the mystery of the eucharist was drawing him ineluctably towards the awesome reality it mediates, the mystery of the Cross into which a Christian is called to enter and participate, sustained by the life and strength given by the Holy Spirit through the sacraments. To this end all Christian life and ministry tend, and therein find their true meaning. By this mystery the unity of the church exists fundamentally unimpaired. Only in this context can the life-giving suffering of Christ's martyr be properly understood as he or she embodies and experiences that which the church believes and exists to make real in every generation. In Ignatius' own words, 'Near to the sword means near to God'. To expose, to endure and to extirpate evil by suffering love is the church's vocation, both corporately and individually, as the Body of Christ in the world.

This is close to the heart of the theology of martyrdom which permeates the book of Revelation, where Jesus Christ is described as 'the faithful witness [Greek *martyros*], the firstborn from the dead and ruler of the kings of the earth' (1:5). From his self-sacrifice upon the Cross springs the liberty and capacity to witness to him even to the point of death. Those who willingly tread this path are revealed as those 'who have passed through the great ordeal; they have washed their robes and made them white in the blood of the Lamb' (7:14). The magnitude and nature of the conflict with evil into which they have been drawn by the power of Christ is indicated as an essentially joyful and victorious struggle: 'By the sacrifice [or blood] of the Lamb and by the witness they bore, they have conquered him; faced with death they did not cling to life' (12:11). This sacrifice is portrayed as participation in the worship of heaven itself.

The account of the martyrdom of St Polycarp (died c. AD 155) illustrates the heavenly dimension graphically. It is one of the most astonishing texts to have survived from the earliest period of Christianity. For his church at Smyrna which recorded it, it was a death 'conformable to the Gospel' pattern, making the truth and glory of the Lord's own passion real and imitable in their own generation.

His impending death did not catch the old man unawares, but rather fully prepared by prayer. He put up a dignified but spirited defence, and was led to the stake to be burned to death. He forbade them to nail him, demanding that they simply tie him, and commended himself to God as a truly living sacrifice. He died as an imitator of his Lord, and as his body baked in a ball of fire, his friends 'perceived a very fragrant odour, as if it were the scent of incense or some other precious spice' (15). Clearly, in the moment of his martyrdom, the sense of the reality and nearness of heaven was palpable and unforgettable. The way of the Cross led truly to the threshold of heaven.

Seldom has persecution been wholly absent from some part of the worldwide church, and in the twentieth century it has proved the bitter yet blessed experience of many Christians under Communist regimes and other forms of dictatorship. From their experience as well as from these earliest Christian testimonies a number of common and salient features emerge: the real presence of Christ himself in the midst of the fear and the pain; the effectiveness of intercession evoked from those being persecuted, even prayer for enemies and torturers; and the sense of the nearness and reality of heaven. For the ultimate threat of evil is to dehumanise, to break the human spirit and will, and so destroy all sense of personal identity and integrity. To this end were concentration camps designed, and therein lay their most fell dread. Only in confronting evil by the power and example of Christ does a person become truly human – a child of God: this is the supreme moment of liberty and likeness to God himself as he became man. Thus the torment becomes a victorious contest, a true ascesis in union with Christ the great Athlete of God. St Athanasius records in his *Life of Antony* how the saint received marked bodily strength as a result of his ferocious tussles with the demons of evil. He emerged from his prolonged time of solitude and suffering, 'initiated into the mysteries, and filled with the Spirit of God', in remarkable physical health and mental well-being, 'wholly guided by reason and abiding in a truly natural state'. The ascetic life which he embodied and exemplified triumphed in the midst of those very spiritual conflicts of which St Paul spoke so clearly in his letters, the conflicts experienced also by the martyrs. For physical torment and persecution are the outward bodily forms *in extremis* of this pattern of permanent but life-giving affliction at the heart of Christian experience, which may truly be described as living through dying.

'Christ was innocent of sin, and yet for our sake God made him one with human sinfulness, so that *in him* we might be made one with the righteousness of God' (2 Cor. 5:21). To be 'in Christ' is, therefore, to experience what Christ endured, the projection of all that evil accomplishes in the hearts of men for the destruction of mankind and God's creation. The mystery of divine love is that by such suffering the Holy Spirit accomplishes in turn the liberation and transformation of human nature, for and through the individual Christian: 'We know that we have crossed over from death to life, because we love our fellow-Christians' (1 John 3:14; cf. John 5:24). This place of judgement and love, the Cross set up in the heart and experience of those who follow Christ and in whom his Spirit dwells, is where the love of God in man for man flows out for the renewal of the church and the healing of mankind and creation. 'The structure of history is *paschal*, in the strict theological sense of 'passover', a passage from this present world into the New Creation' (Patriarch Ignatius IV of Antioch). In the suffering experience of the individual Christian is made real the pattern of God's love at the heart of the church in every place and time, the ceaseless work of him who proclaims, 'I am making all things new' (Rev. 21:5; cf. 2 Cor. 5:17).

Chapter Five

The vision

"We are citizens of heaven."

Chapter 5

The vision

Martyrdom and spiritual vision sprang from the heart of the Jewish religion which gave birth to Christianity. The language of the New Testament clearly has close affinities with contemporary Jewish apocalyptic mysticism. But the language of this spiritual tradition undergoes a complete metamorphosis in the light of the Cross and resurrection of Jesus the heavenly Messiah. Nowhere can this transformation be more closely observed than in Paul's own autobiographical testimony. Jewish apocalyptic mysticism sought a direct and transforming experience of the divine glory, assisted by prayer and asceticism, in terms derived from what were believed to be the spiritual testimonies of the patriarchs and prophets. Paul himself was remembered and portrayed as a man who experienced visions, and not only at the moment of his conversion; there are in fact several such allusions throughout Acts (9:3; 16:9; 18:9; 22:6, 17; 26:13; 27:23). In his letters he frequently speaks about the 'revelation' of the risen Christ upon which he based his entire apostleship (e.g. Gal. 1:12; 2:2). Indeed, he went so far as to declare that his whole experience as a Christian was an act of divine revelation in and through himself, expressed in a life of evangelism and self-sacrifice (Gal. 1:16).

Paul's spiritual authority sprang from his direct and personal encounter with the risen Christ, emphatically recalled in Acts and Galatians. This enabled him to speak so confidently about the reality of resurrection in 1 Corinthians 15, as he boldly associated his own vision of Christ with the tradition of 'appearances' already being handed down in the churches: 'Last of all he appeared to me too' (15:8). His experience was not unique in the New Testament: two others who were suffering for their faith had a similar vision: Stephen in Acts 7:55-6 and the seer John on Patmos in Revelation 1:12ff. The language of each of these visions is highly significant, because Jesus is seen as the heavenly Son of Man, shining with the glory of God. The place of suffering has become the place of vision, the place of encounter with Jesus, the crucified Messiah and the risen Lord. Just as St Paul has articulated the nature and meaning of Christlike suffering, so he is an unique witness to the reality and impact of such a vision.

The language in which Paul articulates his vision is that of Jewish apocalyptic mysticism to which he is a foremost witness in the first century AD. Careful examination reveals that Paul believed that to be 'in Christ' was to experience an actual journey across the threshold to heavenly and eternal life. To be 'in Christ' meant being united to the risen life of Jesus as a body is to its head. Thus the process of actual transformation of the whole human person, including the physical body, lies at the heart of Christianity. Suffering and persecution are 'birth-pangs', which indicate that this process is under way. Resurrection is an inevitable part of Christian belief because it may be experienced here and now as believers enter more deeply into the mystery of Christ. This paschal mystery may be described as living through dying, as earthly life is drawn, in the midst of suffering and weakness, into the orbit of divine life and love. There is enhanced vision, vision of the glory of God in the face of the risen Christ. The vision is life-transforming. It also empowers the mission of the church; for all believers are called to participate in this process, because it constitutes God's saving love at work rescuing mankind, both Jew and Gentile. For unlike both Jewish and Gentile mysticism and ecstatic religion, this road to eternal life is not restricted to the few. In Christ all the hopes and expectations of Jewish apocalyptic mysticism found their fulfilment and transformation. But without the language of that belief and spirituality Paul would have been unable to express his experience of Christ and its meaning.

The most striking and famous passage in which Paul describes this life-transforming vision is in 2 Corinthians 12. He speaks indirectly as if recounting the experience of someone else; this is common in Jewish mystical literature of the time, as is the uncertainty about the precise nature of the 'journey' – 'whether in the body or out of the body' – to the 'third heaven'. Of what he hears he may speak nothing; but out of such experience much may be proclaimed with a new authority and more urgent power. But what is striking about Paul's testimony is that it is hobbled by acute suffering. This is no flight from fleshly existence; rather it is an entering into the mystery of the Cross and resurrection at supreme personal cost. Both vision and suffering are the gift of the Lord, the sign of his nearness and presence. The vision of Christ is not esoteric: the message is very down to earth; 'My grace is all you need; power is most fully seen [or 'perfected'] in weakness' (12:9). There is irony here, for to be 'perfect' as a Christian is to assume a cross, and to this Paul testifies near the close of this letter in 13:4-5: 'you will find that we who share his weakness shall live with him by the power of God'.

The language of transformation is prominent in 2 Corinthians. In chapter 3, Paul affirms the Jewish tradition upon which much mystical theology was built; that the glory of God was in a genuine way reflected in the Law and in Moses' experience of God on Sinai. But it is now eclipsed by the greater and fuller glory which is revealed in Christ: 'we all see as in a mirror the glory of the Lord, and we are being transformed into his likeness with ever-increasing glory, through the power of the Lord who is the Spirit' (3:18). The glory of God is now personified in Christ: he is the 'image of God', the Lord by whom Christians come to experience 'the light which is knowledge of the glory of God in the face of Jesus Christ' (4:6). The force of these words can only be fully weighed against the background of what Paul's Jewish mystical contemporaries believed about the Law and the heavenly realities it mediated in response to human obedience and contemplation. As in the fourth gospel, itself supremely a work of vision, these are bold claims which arise out of the heart of Jewish belief and language, but which transcend and transform them for ever.

The hallmark of this transformation is external sufferings and internal tension, as the earthly body is gradually and painfully subsumed into the heavenly one. This is distinctive language found in other mystical treatises of Jewish provenance. For the believer, 'God has provided ... a house not made by human hands, eternal and in heaven' (5:1). The life of this body will be immortal, and this life is now perceived as a chrysalis in which an irreversible transformation is under way: 'It is for this destiny that God himself has been shaping us; and as a pledge of it he has given us the Spirit' (5:5). Thus in response to suffering, Paul affirms that 'day by day we are inwardly renewed' (4:16). What this signifies is more than simply divine help and comfort in the midst of difficulty. He concludes that 'For anyone united to Christ, there is a new creation: the old order has gone; a new order has already begun' (5:17).

These passages are crucial to the understanding of the heart of Paul's visionary experience. They give direct clues to the nature of his mystical expectation. The vision and the suffering are inextricably conjoined. The light of his testimony in 2 Corinthians illuminates the remaining autobiographical passages in his letters, and throws the language and pattern of his whole theology into the sharpest relief.

The pattern of this 'passing over' from death to life, through suffering to vision, is set forth most fully and poetically in the famous 'Song of Christ's Glory' in Philippians 2:5ff. This may be a very early Christian credal hymn associated with baptism, or it may be Paul's own creation. It is striking in that it indicates the manner in which Christ Jesus, who 'was in the form of God', humbled himself, 'assuming the form of a slave', to the point of crucifixion. 'Therefore God raised him to the heights': Jesus embodies the 'name' of God, to be acclaimed universally as the 'Lord', resplendent in the glory of God. It is a Christology marked by insistence on the heavenly origin of Jesus, the reality of his suffering servanthood, and the pivotal significance of his crucifixion, revealing the eternal meaning of his risen life for the salvation of all mankind. This pattern may readily be discerned throughout the New Testament literature. Paul's own experience of encounter with the risen Christ in the midst of his own sufferings vouched for the authentic, life-giving nature and impact of this belief.

In this very revealing and personal letter to the Philippians, Paul indicates the inner meaning of his belief: contemplating the possibility of impending death, he can affirm 'now as always Christ will display his greatness in me, whether the verdict be life or death. For to me life is Christ, and death is gain' (1:21-2). Later he professes that he has had to lose a great deal of his inherited Jewish religion 'for the sake of gaining Christ and finding myself in union with him' (3:8-9). This union with Christ is the sole basis for justification by faith. He sums up his belief thus: 'My one desire is to know Christ and the power of his resurrection, and to share his sufferings in growing conformity with his death, in hope of somehow attaining the resurrection from the dead' (3:10-11). His hope is kindled and sustained by his experience of the heavenly goal of Christian life; this is the perspective by which all is to be judged.

> We ... are citizens of heaven, and from heaven we expect our deliverer to come, the Lord Jesus Christ. He will transfigure our humble bodies, and give them a form like that of his own glorious body, by that power which enables him to make all things subject to himself. (3:20-1)

This is the heart of how Paul communicated his personal Christian faith and experience to those sympathetic to him. The centrality and total nature of this experience enabled him to speak elsewhere with authority and clarity about the nature of 'that power which enables Christ to make all things subject to himself'.

This power is expressed as love (Christlike love, Greek *agape*). At the close of Romans 8, Paul affirms in a way which can only spring from personal experience that 'nothing in all creation ... can separate us from the love of God in Christ Jesus our Lord' (8:39). The place of the Cross, the place of the cruellest sundering between God and man, is the place of union between God and man, and of reconciliation between man and man. So at the heart of Christian spiritual life, Paul asserts in 1 Corinthians the primacy of love. Its character is Christlike (13:4-7), its nature transcendent, something created in this world which passes into heaven. Growth in love of this kind is the measure and pattern of truly Christian life. The goal is knowledge of God in response to God's loving knowledge of man. Love creates the conditions in which God and man can fully relate, in which human life can be liberated and transformed for ever. Thus the promise of Jesus and the hope of Judaism are fulfilled: 'Blessed are those whose hearts are pure; they shall see God' (Matt. 5:8).

This is why Paul challenges a spirituality which claims special powers. Charismatic 'gifts' of the Spirit may indeed be signs of his presence, but only if they issue in the 'fruits' of the Spirit. These fruits, (listed in Galatians 5:22-3), constitute Christlike love in action in terms of transformed attitudes underlying human relationships. 'Fruits' also are gifts of divine grace, consequences of the Spirit's life within; they are not unaided human achievements. So in Paul's mind the operations of the Spirit are always consistent with this love. The 'power' of the Spirit is not a matter of manipulation or control, or of spiritual display. Instead it interprets the meaning of the diversity of human and spiritual gifts as constituting an organic and growing unity in love and mutual service in the life of the Body of Christ. That Body is a suffering body, not a theatre for self-assertion. Nonetheless Paul reckons with the reality of charismatic signs and gifts as part of life in that Body. But they point beyond themselves to the reality of the Spirit and of eternal life that is mediated by love.

Paul seldom speaks any more directly about his own charismatic experiences than about his contemplative visions; but in Acts he was remembered as a miracle-worker and in 1 Corinthians 2:1-5 he may refer obliquely and idiosyncratically to such events. He certainly has very clear teaching to give about the many gifts of the Spirit in the life of the church, of which the working of miracles is a central and significant part; and it is quite evident that he speaks out of his own experience. A Christian miracle demonstrates the presence of the Holy Spirit, and reveals the way in which human life is being drawn into and transformed by the eternal life and love of God, given in Jesus. By the very nature of that love, a miracle constitutes the healing of a whole person by God, often in ways unexpected, though never unnatural or forced, most often through other people, though they may not always be aware of it. Physical and mental healing are signs and part of an inner spiritual deliverance from evil and renewal of life and love, which is always deeply personal, compassionate and reconciling. A Christian miracle is a proclamation of the gospel, a demonstration of the divine power of love, and of the reality and nearness of eternal life, in defiance of evil; as such it is not wrought without cost. Supremely the cost is God's, for resurrection springs only from Calvary. But often Christians involved in the situation by prayer and service are called to share in that cost through suffering and spiritual conflict. It is against this background, confirmed by his own experience and indicated also by memory of the gospel miracles of Jesus, that Paul speaks when he teaches about the gifts of the Spirit in the life of the church. Although individually experienced and received, these *charismata* have also a corporate character and significance for the life and love of the whole Body of Christ.

The gifts and miracles wrought by the Spirit in the life of the church are crucial signs of the nearness and reality of that new and eternal life in Christ of which Paul speaks. As in the gospels, these are irruptions of divine activity, signalling that the kingdom of God is indeed at hand and present in Christ among men by his Spirit. They indicate too the extent of the transformation of human nature that is possible under the influence of the recreating Spirit of God. They demonstrate also the profound coinherence of the whole church, united as it is by 'the love of God ... shed abroad in our hearts through the Holy Spirit which was given unto us' (Rom. 5:5 RV).

It is because of Paul's continual experience of eternal life here and now that he is able to speak with such confidence in 1 Corinthians 15 about Christian belief in the resurrection. For him the 'traditions' of the appearances of the risen Jesus to his disciples, already history in his time, have been confirmed by his own encounter with the Lord on the Damascus road, and in subsequent spiritual visions also. The little prayer in Aramaic at the very end of this letter, '*Marana tha* – Come, Lord!' (16:22), which found its way into the earliest eucharistic prayer in the *Didache* (10), expresses this hope and expectation of the personal presence of the risen Lord at the heart of the church's worship and prayer. The note is struck in similar form at the end of Revelation (22:20), and sums up the central theme of that book. As in Revelation, so in 1 Corinthians 15 Paul is able to affirm the reality of resurrection in the light of this experience and belief. Christ is indeed raised to life, 'the firstfruits of the harvest of the dead' (15:20). As the heavenly man and saviour he is able to initiate the process whereby those united to him in one Body already begin to pass from death to life, a process brought to completion in eternal life beyond physical death: 'so in Christ all will be brought to life' (15:22). The extent of his lordship is 'until God has put all enemies under his feet', even death itself (15:25-6; cf. Ps. 110:1). Thus the purpose of God will be achieved, and unity through reconciliation accomplished (15:28).

In response to the inevitable question 'How are the dead raised?', Paul adduces the simple parable used also by Jesus in John 12:24 of the seed that has to die in the ground in order to bear a life-giving harvest. Transformation of matter is at the heart of nature; life springs out of death; the universe is made up of radically diverse forms of existence. Thus resurrection is seen as an extension of God's work as creator, recreating *ex nihilo*, but in a genuine and personal continuity arising out of divine love. This Paul vouches for in words that echo his own experience of living through dying:

> So it is with the resurrection of the dead: what is sown as a perishable thing is raised imperishable. Sown in humiliation, it is raised in glory; sown in weakness, it is raised in power; sown a physical body, it is raised a spiritual body. (15:42-4)

The paradox of this assertion is anchored in the history of Calvary, interpreted in the light of the Suffering Servant songs in the prophets and psalms.

He expounds its meaning in words drawn from the language of Jewish apocalyptic mysticism. Christ is the second Adam who inaugurates eternal life for mankind by endowing it with a 'spiritual body' in succession to its 'physical' or 'earthly' one. In Paul's mind this is not simply a metaphor of hope, but a framework for explaining the experience of transformation 'in Christ'. 'The last Adam has become a life-giving spirit' (15:45): therefore, 'As we have worn the likeness of the man made of dust, so we shall wear the likeness of the heavenly man' (15:49). This 'likeness' derives its force from the fundamental doctrine of man made in the image and likeness of God himself in Genesis 1:26-27. As he later indicates in 2 Corinthians 5, this transformation process can be described as a 'clothing' of the body with an immortal nature. Echoing the teaching of Jesus in the gospels, he declares that 'flesh and blood can never possess the kingdom of God, the perishable cannot possess the imperishable' (15:50). There has to be a dying, and that is at the heart of the process as Christians experience it. But the death is not final, and twice he insists that 'we shall all be changed' (15:51 and 52): 'This perishable body must be clothed with the imperishable, and what is mortal with immortality'. In that way the horror of ultimate spiritual and personal destruction for man is overcome: 'Death is swallowed up; victory is won!'

The language of victory – the victory of divine love in human nature and relationships – is seldom far from Paul's lips. Every time he uses the words 'joy' and 'glory' the implications of this vision and experience break through. 'Joy' marks the presence of the Holy Spirit; 'glory' responds to the nearness and presence of the risen Christ: both spur Paul and his hearers on to loving worship of the Father whose purpose and action have made this possible. They constitute the light in which the whole mystery of the church is seen.

The vision of the glory of God in the face of Christ seen by the light of the Spirit is nowhere more fully set forth than in Colossians. Firstly Paul greets the Colossians with great thankfulness and joy (1:3-5). He prays that God may give them 'full insight into his will' and that they may 'give joyful thanks to the Father who has made you fit to share the heritage of God's people in the realm of light' (1:9, 12). The movement from darkness to light is a common metaphor in the New Testament, derived from the Old Testament and gaining special force from the expectations of Jewish mystical prayer. This deliverance constitutes salvation, the sign of which is the forgiveness of sins, which in turn liberates love. Christ is revealed as 'the image of the invisible God; his is the primacy over all creation' (1:15). The mystery at the heart of Christianity is thus that:

> He exists before all things, and all things are held together in him. He is the head of the body, the church. He is its origin, the first to return from the dead, to become in all things supreme. For in him God in all his fullness chose to dwell, and through him to reconcile all things to himself, making peace through the shedding of his blood on the cross – all things, whether on earth or in heaven. (1:17-20)

The implications of these momentous words are spelled out by Paul throughout this letter.

The purpose of God's reconciling work in Christ on the Cross is to restore holiness to men and women, and so to mediate wholeness and peace to the whole created universe. God the creator is God the recreator. Paul's apostleship and vocation is to proclaim this mystery and reality by word and example: 'It is now my joy to suffer for you; for the sake of Christ's body, the church, I am completing what still remains for Christ to suffer in my own person' (1:24). This is the meaning of living through dying. Its goal is a 'wealth of glory' for all mankind, summed up as 'Christ in you, the hope of glory' (1:27), 'in whom lie hidden all the treasures of wisdom and knowledge' (2:3). Christians are called to 'live in union with him' as their Lord (2:6), their hearts 'overflow[ing] with thankfulness' (2:7). 'For it is in Christ that the Godhead in all its fullness dwells embodied, and it is in him that you have been brought to fulfilment' (2:9). As the writer of the fourth gospel declares: 'From his full store we have all received grace upon grace' (John 1:16). To be a Christian is there-fore to 'come to share in the very being of God' himself (2 Pet. 1:4; cf. 1 John 3:2). This is accomplished by baptism, which replaces circumcision as the sign of the new covenant (Colossians 2:11-13), being participation in the mystery of Christ's death and resurrection (cf. Rom. 6:1-11). In Christ alone is found the true spiritual reality which is life-giving. This reality is heaven, the kingdom of God's eternal life and love, to which Christ leads. Paul concludes: 'You died; and now your life lies hidden with Christ in God. When Christ, who is our life, is revealed, then you too will be revealed with him in glory' (3:3-4).

In the meantime, and as part of that reality, the life in Christ is revealed in the life and nature of the church, and the new pattern of values, attitudes and relationships between people of all backgrounds nurtured there. The suffering and the vision turn outwards to the world that God through man is seeking to save by love.

Chapter Six

The Body

"Faith expressing itself through love."

Chapter 6

The Body

Baptism constitutes life in the Body of Christ, the church and the church exists to sustain Christians in that experience of living through dying which is the mystery at the heart of its life. To the Colossians Paul declares: 'you were buried with him in baptism, and in that baptism you were also raised to life with him through your faith in the active power of God, who raised him from the dead' (Col. 2:12). By this Christians experience liberation from and forgiveness of their sins – the direct consequence of the reconciling power of Calvary. The full meaning of this central belief is spelled out by Paul in Romans 6:1-14. Here Paul reiterates firstly his teaching in Colossians: baptism unites a person to the dying and rising of Jesus. This mystery contains the hope of final resurrection to an eternal life; it also sheds light on how a Christian must live and why:

> We know that our old humanity has been crucified with Christ,
> for the destruction of the sinful self, so that we may no longer
> be slaves to sin ... you must regard yourselves as dead to sin
> and alive to God, in union with Christ Jesus. (6:6, 11)

God's grace enables a Christian gradually no longer to have to sin, and in the process a personality is healed, liberated and restored to its original integrity. Whereas 'sin pays a wage, and the wage is death ... God gives freely, and his gift is eternal life in union with Christ Jesus our Lord' (6:23). Built upon faith and expressed in love, this is a new relationship, or covenant, with God, sustained by the very life and grace of God himself, given through Christ by the Spirit. Baptism, therefore, determines the whole pattern of Christian living, and the meaning of suffering also. The road of living through dying is an inescapable consequence of participation in this mystery.

Participation in the mystery of the dying and rising of Christ is renewed in every eucharist. Paul makes the connection explicit in 1 Corinthians 10, by reference to the exodus story, interpreted as 'baptism into the fellowship of Moses in cloud and sea. They all ate the same supernatural food, and all drank of the same supernatural drink' (10:2-3). In this old covenant, Christ himself was giving himself to his people. Then in relation to the vexed issue of participation in food offered to idols, Paul upholds the ban for Christians by reference to the eucharist:

> When we bless the cup of blessing, is it not a means of sharing in the blood of Christ? When we break the bread, is it not a means of sharing in the body of Christ? Because there is one loaf, we, though many, are one body; for it is one loaf of which we all partake. (10:16-17)

These are important words for understanding the earliest belief about the eucharist, found also in the *Didache* (9), where there is the prayer: 'As this broken bread was scattered upon the mountains and being gathered together became one, so may your church be gathered together from the ends of the earth into your kingdom'. The eucharist constitutes the unity of the church in a common experience of living through dying, of participation in the mystery of the crucified and risen Christ. Paul, therefore, emphasises Christ's own words of institution, concluding that 'every time you eat this bread and drink the cup, you proclaim the death of the Lord, until he comes' (11:26). So awesome and immediate is this reality, that to participate in the eucharist 'unworthily' is to experience judgement, 'if a person does not discern the body' (11:29). Thus the eucharist is the wellspring of all Christian relationships, and to be unreconciled there is a denial and destructive (cf. Matt. 5:23-24). It affirms and expresses again and again the whole movement in Christian life and experience from darkness to light, from death to life, through dying to sin and self to newness of life in Christ. The eucharist is the paschal mystery which is entering into union with Christ himself by means of his own self-giving (cf. 1 Cor. 5:7). It is the indwelling of the Holy Spirit that makes this union possible.

It is in Romans 8 that Paul sets forth most clearly his understanding of the Holy Spirit. Those who are 'united with Christ Jesus' are freed from fear of condemnation because 'In Christ Jesus the life-giving law of the Spirit has set you free from the law of sin and death' (8:1-2). The Spirit is described by Paul as the Spirit of God and also of Christ: 'You live by the Spirit, since God's Spirit dwells in you' (8:9). This is the basis and meaning of justification by faith, 'Christ is in you', and herein lies the hope also of ultimate resurrection (8:10-11). 'All who are led by the Spirit of God are sons of God' (8:14ff.), which means a relationship of love, freedom and trust – the abolition of fear and slavery. 'The Spirit affirms to our spirit that we are God's children; and if children, then heirs, heirs of God and fellow-heirs with Christ' (8:16-17). In Galatians, Paul draws out the important implications of this belief for the Christian understanding of humanity:

> It is through faith that you are all sons of God in union with Christ Jesus. Baptized into union with him, you have all put on Christ like a garment. There is no such thing as Jew and Greek, slave and freeman, male and female; for you are all one in Christ Jesus. (3:26-28)

In both these contexts, Paul makes a rare but direct allusion to the distinctive way in which Jesus addressed God as 'Abba – Father'. For in Romans 8, he returns to the fundamental theme of suffering as a hallmark of sonship: 'but we must share his sufferings if we are also to share his glory' (8:17). The sufferings manifest the glory; and the glory illuminates the whole meaning of the sufferings for mankind and for the whole created order; and it is the Spirit who holds the two together within the heart of a Christian's life.

Paul believes that 'the sufferings we now endure bear no comparison with the glory, as yet unrevealed, which is in store for us' (8:18). He uses the metaphor of childbirth to describe how the sufferings of the church lie at the heart of the suffering in the world, including the created order. Conjoined to mankind, and affected by sinfulness, the 'whole created universe in all its parts groans as if in the pangs of childbirth', called as it is 'to enter upon the glorious liberty of the children of God' (8:21-22). This is the meaning of the references elsewhere in Paul's writings to the *cosmic* scope of salvation in Christ. The fall and redemption of man have revealed the inner purpose and working of God as creator and recreator: all matter, all flesh can become God-bearing by the indwelling of the Holy Spirit; and the reality and tendency of that indwelling is experienced at the heart of Christian life.

Paul then describes vividly his own experience of prayer, the knowledge of the Spirit's activity within him in the midst of suffering and weakness. The Spirit prays through his 'inarticulate groans', despite the sense of ignorance of how to pray. Instead a person finds himself *within* the will of God, caught up in the loving communication and mercy which abide within the heart and nature of God himself. This praying purpose of God in man for man is so sure that Paul can affirm that 'in everything [the Spirit] co-operates for good with those who love God and are called according to his purpose' (8:28). The Christians is called thus to become by divine grace what Christ was by nature, 'to share the likeness of God's Son', to become a person in whom God the Spirit prays, through whom God is able to love himself and mankind. Following the path of the praying and suffering Christ, the Christian discovers that, sustained by the Spirit within in the midst of afflictions, 'nothing in all creation ... can separate us from the love of God in Christ Jesus our Lord' (8:39).

The experience of the indwelling of the Holy Spirit is the bond of love which sustains the life and integrity of the church. This divine love in human nature is the well-spring of Christian ethics. In 1 Corinthians on two occasions Paul affirms that the human person, the human body, is designed and intended by God to become the 'sanctuary' in which the Holy Spirit can dwell. 'Surely you know that you are God's temple, where the Spirit of God dwells ... the temple of God is holy; and you are that temple' (3:16-17). Here he is affirming the principle of accountability to God for the kind of life a person lives.

Do you not know that your bodies are limbs and organs of Christ? ... Do you not know that your body is a temple of the indwelling Holy Spirit, and the Spirit is God's gift to you? You do not belong to yourselves; you were bought at a price. Then honour God in your body. (6:15, 19-20)

Here Paul is tackling the perennial issue of sexuality and its legitimate expression, reminding his hearers that, as in the Old Testament, fornication is a sin against both God and man. The sense of God's own indwelling Spirit, his personal presence and love, must determine the whole spirit of Christian behaviour towards everyone.

The sense of the Spirit's indwelling makes intelligible the whole approach of Christians to prayer. It is something that we will God to accomplish in and through us; we offer him ourselves as a simple whole. In love for Christ, we let our mind and our will be led by the Spirit into the heart of our person, there to encounter the reality of God himself. The sense of his presence there liberates a very great love which sustains our whole life. As in the words of Jesus in St John's gospel: 'The water that I shall give will be a spring of water within him, welling up and bringing eternal life' (John 4:14). This is that 'living sacrifice' of which the eucharist speaks, a living sacrifice that is also life-giving to others. This joyful self-sacrifice to God in love and freedom is our response to his self-giving to us in Christ and in the Holy Spirit. From this movement of the heart and will is derived that principle of strict accountability for all we do and are, and for the whole way we relate to other people. We begin to see others in the light of God's deep love for them as well as for ourselves.

The simplicity and wholeness of Christian self-offering in the power of the Spirit, and the loving sense of accountability it induces, constitute chastity. God's purpose is to restore to man complete personality, and personality subsists in and is fulfilled by relationships; also true relationships can only exist between whole persons whose lives are conduits of love, freedom and trust. All human relationships flow from a person's relationship to God: that is why the great commandment conjoins love of God and love of neighbour. True love of neighbour is Christlike in the sense that it is based upon self-sacrifice and self-giving, even to the point of love of enemies. This is the 'new' commandment of the gospels, demonstrated and vindicated in the life and sufferings of Jesus. A person's life is bodily, and so how we relate to others in their bodily existence, and indeed to material things in general, matters fundamentally. Human sexuality is by its nature something life-giving and loving, an expression of self-giving and self-sacrifice, both towards the partner and towards the children yet to be. In a unique way it mirrors and participates in the creative life-giving love that is at the heart of God. Its uniqueness in marriage is its strength and the clue to its deepest meaning. For as Paul shows in Ephesians 5:21-33, a Christian marriage mirrors and gives access to the mystery at the heart of the church's life of how Christ relates to mankind. A Christian marriage must be filled with a Christlike love, tried and tested by a lifetime's forgiveness and self-giving, the focal point for a whole web of relationships guided and sustained by that same love.

The ethos of this love permeates the moral teaching with which Paul concludes so many of his letters. In Romans, for example, he summarises his approach in two notable passages. In 12:1-2 he urges his hearers:

by God's mercy to offer your very selves to him: a living sacrifice, dedicated and fit for his acceptance, the worship offered by mind and heart. Conform no longer to the pattern of this present world, but be transformed by the renewal of your minds. Then you will be able to discern the will of God, and to know what is good, acceptable, and perfect.

He proceeds to spell out the practical meaning of this in relation to a whole range of issues in a manner close in spirit to the teaching of Jesus in the gospels. At the heart of it all is the principle:

For none of us lives, and equally none of us dies, for himself alone. If we live, we live for the Lord; and if we die, we die for the Lord ... we belong to the Lord ... each of us will be answerable to God. (14:7-8, 12)

This is most evident in the subtle and sensitive way in which Paul elaborates his understanding of the church as the Body of Christ in 1 Corinthians 12. It arises out of his consideration of the meaning of the eucharist in the previous chapter, with its warning about the need to 'discern the body' – the real presence of Christ in the midst of his people in the sacrament. The indwelling of the Spirit through faith and baptism enables the basic Christian profession, 'Jesus is Lord' (12:3). The gift of the Spirit is to the individual within the life of the Body; there is, therefore, a diversity of gifts but a single purpose in love sustained by the one Spirit: 'all these gifts are the activity of one and the same Spirit, distributing them to each individual at will' (12:11). One Spirit unites believers of all racial, social and religious backgrounds, men and women equally, into the one Body of Christ. With great irony, Paul portrays the several members of the body, each one indispensable in its unique function, so ridiculing any centrifugal or self-assertive tendencies among Christians. He emphasises that often the frailer parts are the more vital, and reminds the hearers of the special care shown towards those parts of the body regarded as 'less honourable'. 'God has combined the various parts of the body, giving special honour to the humbler parts' (12:24). The unity of the body is expressed by the mutual care of each for each and all: indeed, 'If one part suffers, all suffer together; if one flourishes, all rejoice together' (12:26). This bond of compassion is the true hallmark of the church's life, the expression of its hidden unity and deep fellowship throughout the world. It is something which transcends the merely human historical and cultural differences which mark the various institutional expressions of the church's life in the world. It is truly the sign of reconciliation and restoration to a divided humanity, the indication of God's saving love and presence in history and society at any time.

The life and organisation of any institutional expression of the church is authentic and life-giving only in so far as it is truly guided and moulded by this Christlike love, this sense of solidarity and compassion as the Body of Christ. Central to whether this is so is the way authority and leadership are exercised. There are in the New Testament two dominant images of pastoral and apostolic authority, both drawn from the example of Jesus himself: the Shepherd and the Servant. In the letters of St Paul it is possible to see how this style of authority operated, and it is quite clear that such pastoral authority rested upon prayer, example and suffering. There was neither the scope nor the inclination to exercise any coercive power, even if at times Paul could be very forceful in what he said and how he said it. Indeed, there are many occasions when it is the virtual powerlessness of the apostle in the face of distant problems and misunderstandings which is the most striking feature of his appeal to the churches.

How Paul felt about his own predicament as a Christian leader is made quite clear in 2 Corinthians 11:28-29: 'Apart from these external things [i.e. afflictions], there is the responsibility that weighs on me every day, my anxious concern for all the churches'. It was this burning care which motivated him to write so directly to churches with which he had been involved, and even to churches he had not yet visited, such as that at Rome. In Paul's mind, pastoral care and mission went together, and a Christian leader was directly answerable to God for his ministry: 'We are to be regarded as Christ's subordinates and as stewards of the secrets of God. Now stewards are required to show themselves trustworthy' (1 Cor. 4:1-2). That Paul takes the reality of divine judgement very seriously in this matter is quite evident later in the same letter: 'I do not spare my body, but bring it under strict control, for fear that after preaching to others I should find myself disqualified' (9:27). This conviction of strict accountability towards God colours also the way he deals with those whom he regards as 'false brethren' masquerading as leaders in the churches. His teaching is the same as that of Jesus in the gospels: it is by their fruits that they may be recognised for what they are.

At the same time, Paul sees himself as profoundly accountable to the churches to whom he writes and whom he seeks to serve, not perhaps for the source of his authority as an apostle and pastor, but certainly for its integrity and credibility. Again and again he appeals to their memory of him as a person, and to the meaning of his own Christian example. For example, in defending an earlier letter to Corinth in 2 Corinthians 2:4, Paul asserts:

that letter I sent you came out of great distress and anxiety; how many tears I shed as I wrote it! Not because I wanted to cause you pain; rather I wanted you to know the love, the more than ordinary love, that I have for you.

This captures well the spirit in which he wrote, and accounts for his unusual frankness and feeling. He saw himself as a spiritual father to those churches which he had brought into being (cf. 1 Cor. 4:15-16; Gal. 4:19). Frequently he reminds his hearers of the free and open approach he adopted among them, refusing rhetoric, deceit or manipulation, or any form of economic exploitation of them. Instead the heart of his approach is encapsulated in these words from 2 Corinthians 4:5: 'It is not ourselves that we proclaim: we proclaim Christ Jesus as Lord, and ourselves as your servants for Jesus's sake'. Paul takes the theme of being a 'servant', or more precisely a 'slave', very seriously, and 'the slave of Christ' is one of his own self-designations (cf. Rom. 1:1; Gal. 1:10). It lies close to the heart of his own understanding of the coming of Christ who assumed 'the form of a slave' (Phil. 2:7). It gave him a lively sympathy with Christian slaves like Philemon, and enabled him to challenge directly one of the most deep-rooted social attitudes of his day, that towards slavery itself, in Ephesians 6:5-9. In this passage is contained his whole theology of man and therefore of authority itself, now in obedience to Christ. It is not only a potent challenge in the long term to the social order built upon slavery; far more radically, it injects a genuine humanity back into all existing social relationships, a bond of mutual human accountability which springs from an equal accountability and value as persons before God himself.

The whole of 2 Corinthians is exercised by the question of Paul's authority and its meaning for the church to which he is writing, which is itself convulsed by a breakdown of spiritual authority of a uniting kind. In the last chapter, Paul defines Christian authority in two ways: in 13:8, he asserts that, 'We have no power to act against the truth, but only for it'; in 13:10, he defines authority as 'authority which the Lord gave me for building up and not for pulling down'. At the heart of the word 'authority' lies the sense of something life-giving, something shared and given away, often at great personal cost. As such it has also to be received, for Christian authority rests upon and enhances personal freedom. In a sense, any real Christian leadership has to be permitted and enabled to function, as it cannot coerce its way. The relative 'powerlessness' of this situation is the peculiar burden placed upon the Christian leader or minister, especially as he or she has to contend with the doleful consequences in any church or community which refuses to accept authority. Yet as is made explicit in St John's gospel, this burden of 'powerlessness' was Christ's also: 'Remember what I said: "A servant is not greater than his master." If they persecuted me, they will also persecute you; if they have followed my teaching, they will follow yours' (John 15:20).

Paul's testimony is vivid insight into the trials of Christian leadership, that suffering which in fact gives life and form to the Body of Christ, the church. Paul the 'slave of Christ' is under direct obedience to God as pastor and apostle. As 'shepherd', as the Lord's representative in relation to the churches, the burden of care is his, and it is a painful, costly and at times frustrating one. He must face the spiritual conflict, often alone, and warn against the machinations and deceits of evil in human guise, not least among other so-called Christian leaders and ministers. Like his Lord, he is in a real sense 'powerless', easily ignored and humiliated. Thus the true 'servant' (or slave) is revealed, who can use only the 'weapons' of love: truthfulness, persuasion, prayer, compassion and courageous example. In such a way does the Christian leader discharge the ministry of the Lord himself to his own Body.

'Love is patient and kind' (1 Cor. 13:4), and the Christian apostle and pastor must embody and pursue the purposeful patience and unfailing kindness of God himself as revealed in Jesus. He or she will be able to do this only by entering deeply into the dying and living of Christ, and so beginning to detect, from the standpoint of divine purpose and patience, how God's love works, and wherein lies its mysterious power; and to discern also that pattern of living through dying already under way in the lives of those whom God has committed to his or her care. To be a Christian leader or minister is, therefore, to be a fellow-worker with the Holy Spirit in his cure of souls; and his way is always the working of love, both in judgement and compassion, until the Body, individually and corporately, comes to have the form of Christ himself who is its head.

Chapter Seven

The call

"Christ in you, the hope of glory."

Chapter 7

The call

The spiritual experience which St Paul was the first to describe from within lies at the heart of all Christian experience in every age and place. He describes it as being 'in Christ', and so entering into his dying and rising. He speaks also of being conscious of the indwelling of the Holy Spirit, and standing upon the threshold of eternal life. For this reason Paul has been regarded by many spiritual writers of the church as their spiritual father. His language gave them the spring-board for expressing further the mystery of Christ and of life in the Spirit. His testimony gave them, in terms verifiable by their own experience, an important key to the kingdom of heaven, because it was a framework capable of interpreting the meaning of the spiritual sufferings which assailed them as they advanced in prayer.

For it is the prerequisite of growth in Christian prayer and living to accept the reality and inevitability of spiritual suffering for the sake of Christ. Such suffering is passive and can neither be controlled nor mitigated, and such can be its subtle force that it may seem to threaten the very identity and stability of a person for a time. In a society which increasingly, and rightly, tries to control and subdue pain, whether physical or mental, this may seem a paradoxical prospect. But the way to Christ lies through intense spiritual suffering, to be personally endured. Only this can open our eyes to the deeper meaning of the Scriptures and the testimonies of the saints. On the way our own sympathy and compassion for all other sufferers and suffering societies are transformed in a manner otherwise un-imaginable, and perhaps unattainable also. Suffering is one of the fundamental common bonds between human beings and between churches. It is central to the call of the gospel, and as such it cuts against the grain of many of the basic assumptions of modern society in the west. The challenge is above all to our own free will: it is a willing handing over of our persons to the will of God, wherever that may lead us. We know that in the end, and by a path as yet unforeseen, the will of God will lead us to the Cross – and beyond.

The principal cause of this spiritual suffering is evil, seeking to dominate the human mind and so to manipulate the heart and will towards destructive ends. Here again St Paul is adamant and direct: there is an acute conflict at the heart of Christianity, which never ends completely in this life. Vulnerability to the machinations of evil, often working through the unkindness of fellow human beings, is inescapable in the following of Christ. Earlier generations had a surer framework by which to account for this pressing reality, a demonology which, while it expressed itself in vivid images, none the less conveyed in an accurate and comprehensive way what actually happens to a Christian who truly prays. Not to reckon with the reality of evil and its implacable hostility towards both God and mankind is to walk across a battlefield as if on the way to a picnic! It is also naive in the light of the many horrors of the twentieth century alone.

The problem of evil crushes many human spirits inside and outside the church. It is vital for all Christians, both in their prayers and in their compassion for others, to know their enemy and to be aware of the kind of hold evil can exert in human affairs. Prayer reveals the nature and nearness of evil; it also illumines the inner nature of Christ's own passion, the reason why the gospel account of his ministry and destiny is as it is. The Cross demonstrates in stark horror where evil wills to lead man: to the contempt of God in the destruction of his fellow-man. This is a terrible truth which searches the hearts of all men and women all the time. There is in Christian prayer no shirking this tragedy which darkens the hearts of all born into this world. The light shines into the darkness of our hearts, revealing and in the end destroying the darkness, if we will it so to do. Without this light of Christ within, the way back to God could never be found or followed.

Central to the gospel is the Cross. St Paul's own testimony gives meaning to the cryptic call of Jesus in the gospels to his own disciples to 'take up the cross daily' and only so to follow him. In its day it was an astonishing, even shocking, metaphor. Today in western society its meaning may seem paradoxical, even unattainable. But the road of Christian prayer and service soon lays its own cross upon a Christian, in terms of irksome suffering, frustrating relationships, malignant opposition, or dark oppression directly by evil itself. Again, an indirect consequence of this is a deeper understanding and love for those many of our fellow-men across the world for whom life feels an actual cross, an inescapable burden and humiliation; for whom independence and self-assertion are mirages without meaning or hope. This is the common lot of too many; yet the gospel of Jesus proclaims the nearness of God especially to them.

Gradually the taking up of the cross in daily prayer and self-sacrificial love draws us to the place of the Cross itself, where God meets man in Christ. Revealed and established in history, the Cross is none the less the place of ultimate spiritual reality, in the sense that it is the focal point of our human experience in this life, and of our praying and our following of Christ. By it all life is measured; towards it the yearning and sufferings of the heart of love are directed. It is an empty Cross because it is also the place of resurrection, the trysting-place with the risen Christ who makes himself known in a real and personal way to all who seek him there. Around this place the path of living through dying circles, drawing ever deeper into the mystery of Christ himself.

There is in Christian prayer a genuine dying to self which comes when a person feels himself to be on the Cross with Christ in some indescribable way. Powerlessness and humiliation at the hands of evil itself, sometimes working through adverse human circumstances and relationships, strip the self of all sense of worth, dignity and freedom. Can God be in such an hour of darkness? Yet to be with Christ on the Cross of his suffering is to be very close to the mystery of divine love at work redeeming the lost world of mankind. With Christ in hell, hell is conquered. So the place of dying becomes the place of resurrection; where life is laid down, life is restored and renewed. Beneath the shadow of the Cross lies the empty tomb, the open door of which is in fact the threshold of heaven and the conduit through which the eternal life of God himself enters human nature. For this way of the Cross, St Paul remains the surest guide.

So Christians in every generation must recover those real thresholds of eternity, open to man in Christ where, in the words of T.S. Eliot, 'prayer has been valid'. Most obviously these are the places made holy by saints, saturated still by their hidden presence and prayerful love. In Eliot's words again:

But to apprehend the point of intersection of the timeless with time, is an occupation for the saint – no occupation either, but something given and taken, in a lifetime's death in love, ardour and selflessness and self-surrender. (*The Dry Salvages* V)

But there are other thresholds of eternity too: the altar of the eucharist, where the flame of the Spirit descends and Christ gives himself in the communion of his saints; and the altar in the depths of the human heart at prayer, where the indwelling Spirit intimates the divine love and presence.

The nearness and accessibility of eternity is the joyful mystery at the heart of Christianity, the new life in Christ mediated by the Spirit which remakes and transforms human nature itself. The good news is that humanity can be liberated and made whole. The experience of this is energised by worship and prayer, by hearts and minds open to God and responsive to his love. Worship means self-giving to God in response to his self-giving to us; it entails single-minded and open-hearted self-forgetfulness in the presence of God, and in com-passionate intercession for others. This is what generates Christian fellowship and mediates the reality of Christ and the Holy Spirit to those who come within its influence. It is a transforming experience, a gift of divine grace poured out, to be received gladly and freely, but never in a way that is manipulative or self-gratifying.

It is the language of Scripture and of Christian tradition which mediates to us the reality it indicates and describes. Christian theology and liturgy exist to draw men and women into an experience of the living God, which will change their lives. We are called to live within a great and living tradition of Christian witness, for as Eliot wrote: 'the communication of the dead is tongued with fire beyond the language of the living' (*Little Gidding* I). Such words are living words which communicate an immediate experience available in every place and time to men and women, because those who uttered them live unto God, and the experience to which they point is that of the living God who revealed himself as 'I AM' to Moses at the burning bush. That is how Jesus rebuffed the scepticism of the Sadducees, who distanced the primordial religious experience of Israel and denied the possibility of resurrection: 'God is not God of the dead but of the living' (Mark 12:27). So in our day it is false historicism to render the language of Scripture and tradition as relative and remote, sundered from that of our time by the progress or otherwise of history. Of course the language used by former generations is coloured and formed by a precise historical and cultural context. This is susceptible to study and apprehension. But, in Christian tradition from the earliest times, what is remarkable to observe, as in the spiritual testimony of St Paul himself, is the transformation of language and imagery in order to express in precise terms an experience arising out of and in response to a definite historical happening and person, Christ, through whom the reality and nature of God was seen in a new and transforming light. Thus the heart of Christian experience in any church tradition, age and circumstance reveals the same pattern of transformed language in response to the living person through whom God becomes real. There is, therefore, a common language of Christian experience which mediates that experience in a way that is striking both by its inherent unity and its rich diversity.

The transformation of human nature and language is the work of the Holy Spirit, who brings people into a community which is in union with the living Christ. This is the central and most determining experience at the heart of Christianity, and that which makes the gospel urgently relevant to the sinful, suffering, tragic world of mankind. The church exists to create within itself the conditions where this can happen, and be sustained and made accessible to various human societies. The task of any institutional church is to conform its common life, organisation and worship to the spiritual reality of the church which the Holy Spirit is creating in its midst. It is of course tragically possible for the life of an institutional church, deliberately or by neglect, to fall away from this vocation. But this is its vocation – to be a true fellow-worker with the Holy Spirit in his mission of saving love towards mankind. This is a daunting and searching task laid upon all Christians, which when properly faced dispels any complacency about the relative success of church life and activity.

> His path has been trodden from the ages and from all generations by the Cross and by death. But how is it with you, that the afflictions on the path seem to you to be off the path? Do you not wish to follow the steps of the saints? Or have you plans for devising some new way of your own, and of journeying therein without suffering? The path of God is a daily Cross. No-one has ascended into heaven by means of ease: in truth, without afflictions, there is no Life.

These challenging words of St Isaac the Syrian, who died in the seventh century, echo the authentic call of the gospel: 'Anyone who wants to be a follower of mine must renounce self; he must take up his cross and follow me' (Mark 8:34). There is no other way to eternal life: 'narrow is the gate and constricted the road that leads to life, and those who find them are few' (Matt. 7:14). This way is found in Jesus: 'I am the way, the truth, and the life; no one comes to the Father except by me' (John 14:6).

The reality of the Cross must stand at the heart of a church's life, because the church is the Body of Christ united to its head in his death and resurrection. Upon the Cross, the whole truth about man in relationship to God converges. There the true nature and awfulness of evil is revealed. The Cross interprets what is happening in all places of cruelty and evil in human life today. It strips away illusions about human motives and actions, and discloses the murderous intentions of evil towards humanity. It is the one secure point of reference for all human conduct at any level.

The Cross is the place of liberation. From fear of the power of evil, because upon the rock of Christ's humanity the force of evil overreached itself and was shattered. From sinfulness, as the depth and extent of God's love for human beings is revealed in all its cost. From guilt, because the death of Christ was a sacrifice: each Christian may feel truly that 'he died for me'. From cowardice, because wickedness unresisted will destroy both body and soul, whereas there is no greater love than to lay down one's life for others. From self-pity, because suffering accepted for the sake of God is the bond of love that unites Christians to their Lord and to each other.

It is, therefore, very wrong to remove from the language of the Cross its saving power, and to regard 'the blood of Christ' or 'his sacrifice' as simply metaphors. They are true symbols in the sense that they communicate to those who receive them the power of the reality they describe. By word, deed and suffering God reaches man at the depths of his failure, need and vulnerability. Such words convey to the heart and mind of a person what God has done for humanity in Christ, but in a deeply personal way which transforms life from within irreversibly. The reality and significance of the Cross are the foundation also of the corporate life of the church.

The foundation of the church's life is revealed in baptism, and for any church to function and flourish, the meaning of baptism must be set forth and experienced repeatedly. The life of Christians needs to be related to the baptism they have received, whether as children or adults. Although the church is in the world, it is not of the world. There has to be a passing over from an old life to a new, and this means in part from one lifestyle to another. There has to be recognition that Christian hopes and values are distinct and at times at variance with those of non-Christians. There is a qualitative difference between 'darkness' and 'light': even though Christians do not claim to be wholly light, it is towards the light of God's goodness revealed in Christ that they are travelling, leaving what is dark and corrupt behind them. There has also to be an acceptance of inner cleansing by a living God:

> If we claim to be sinless, we are self-deceived and the truth is not in us. If we confess our sins, he is just and may be trusted to forgive our sins and cleanse us from every kind of wrongdoing. (1 John 1:8-9)

Christians need to be very clear-headed about what is right and wrong, and must not think that deliberate sin is at all compatible with life in Christ. Because baptism opens the door of the human heart to the indwelling of the Holy Spirit, the body becomes the sanctuary of the Spirit, and a sanctuary must by its nature be undefiled.

Baptism sets the basic rhythm of Christian life, the spiral path of divine love that determines all our days. It orientates Christians to hear the voice of divine love calling persons and communities into a deeper communion. The voice of divine calling is heard supremely through the Scriptures, and that is the root of their authority for Christian living. It is, therefore, a profound mistake for a church to fail to take seriously the language and authority of Scripture. The 'many and varied ways' by which the Scriptures speak find their point of unity in the person of Christ himself (cf. Heb. 1:1-2). Language is the means of communication between persons, and the meaning and reliability of the words of Scripture, the truth of the Bible, are verified in the experience of God in Christ which individuals and communities encounter. The inspiration of Scripture means that the same mind operates throughout, the mind of the Holy Spirit. In the Bible the mind of God interacts with the mind of man, in history and also in the present. As in the story of the burning bush, God identifies himself as 'I AM', for 'in his sight all are alive' (Luke 20:38). We are called through the testimony of the Bible to relate to his eternal reality.

To place the 'many and varied ways' of the Scriptures in their precise historical context is important. But it is preliminary and subordinate to hearing the consistent voice of the living God throughout their pages, who by addressing men then, addresses them now as well. To drive a wedge between the Old and New Testaments, or between the fourth gospel and the synoptics, for example, is to deny this truth and reality which has been central to the tradition of the church in every age. The Word of God is expressed supremely in the person of Christ, and the wider Scriptures are the context in which that truth can be seen and apprehended.

The meaning of baptism and the authority of Scripture find their focus in the eucharist, which constitutes the heart of the church's life. Here, word and action are united in the person of Christ who gives himself to the church, to persons in communion with him and with each other. The eucharist mediates to Christians the reality of eternal life. It is, therefore, both a celebration and a participation in the resurrection. It is central to the life of the church because the church exists to make possible this life-transforming experience to mankind. This vocation is set forth before Christians every time this sacrament is celebrated: in the offering and hallowing of the bread and the wine the church sees what it is to become, and by communion begins to become more what it truly is. It is important, therefore, that nothing should happen in Christian worship, especially at the eucharist, that might distract from this reality. The test of the impact of that reality is in worship characterised by holiness, and relationships hallmarked by self-sacrificial love. This is why barriers to inter-communion between baptised christians are so deplorable.

This sacramental life springs from the Incarnation – the belief that in Jesus God became man. The highest thing that a person may give in love is himself or herself, as in marriage. God gave no less than himself for the salvation and sanctification of mankind. His uniqueness expressed itself in a unique personality, Jesus. He was a truly human being, both in the sense of actual historical existence and because, made in the image and likeness of God and unsullied by sin, he reveals to man truly what it means to be a human being in union with God. It is, therefore, a fatal mistake in any way to diminish the actuality of his historical existence, or to cast doubt upon the ancient testimonies as to how his life began and ended. To regard the accounts of his conception and birth as inspired fable is to raise great, if not insuperable, historical difficulties, which undermine the reliability of the gospels as a whole. It is also to miss the truth about the depth of the divine union with every stage of human existence from conception to death, and beyond. The resurrection of Jesus is about a personal divine reality endowed with eternal life to whom those who knew him could relate directly. The reality of this personal existence has been further confirmed by many experiences of the risen Christ since the days of the New Testament. For humans to be personal means being bodily as well: the actuality of the empty tomb and the manner of Christ's first appearances point to the full reality of that resurrection, which was bodily because it was per-sonal. At the heart of Christianity in any age lies a deep personal and corporate loyalty, love and worship towards a Lord who is alive and real.

She who bore this Incarnation is the foremost indicator as to its meaning for the whole life of mankind. 'The Holy Spirit will come upon you, and the power of the Most High will overshadow you' (Luke 1:35). The Virgin Mary is described as the 'God-bearer'. As a consequence of the Incarnation it is possible for human nature, saved and sanctified by God in Christ, itself to become 'God-bearing', to become filled by the Holy Spirit. The presence of the Spirit restores a person in the image and the likeness of God until that personality, in all its uniqueness, becomes a bright reflection and expression of the invisible, Christ-like God. That is the goal of Christian life, and the process begins now in time and history.

Christians believe that human beings were created to 'share in the very being of God' (2 Pet. 1:4), for in the words of St Augustine: 'you made us for yourself and our hearts find no peace until they rest in you' (*Confessions* I:1). The structure of the human heart, which is the well-spring of our being, is designed to be indwelt by the Holy Spirit of God. The way to that deep place within is way-marked by prayer, suffering and self-surrender. It is the road of living through dying, where the conflicts which culminated upon Calvary are discovered to rage also in the heart of each person. The battleground between good and evil is found there, and all external conflict or oppression is a projection of that inner disease. This is the meaning of original sin. It is also an indicator of the profound coinherence which binds all humanity together. For there is often a linkage between external difficulties and inner struggles and pain. Deeper than the obvious tussle between mind and heart is the battle for the human will. Here lies the root of sin, and the most potent reminder of human frailty. The will's stability and direction are the foundation of that inner sense of identity and purpose without which human life is demoralised and lost.

So the inner spiritual conflict with evil and temptation, to which St Paul bears such eloquent testimony, is in microcosm part of the wider tragedy of man which none may escape. Calvary is discovered to be at the heart of man's existence, with the foot of the Cross planted firmly in hell. The path of living through dying is indeed a fearsome descent within. But it is a path of the living – the only path for those who would truly live. As St Seraphim of Sarov said: 'Have peace in yourself, and thousands around you will be saved'. For in the human heart the fall of man may be checked and turned by Christ himself.

This checking and turning is a lifetime's endeavour of love, with which we cooperate through prayer. In baptism, Christ the Light descends into our darkness within, and with our consent begins to banish the gloom of sin and evil throughout the labyrinthine passages of the heart. Each time we receive the eucharist this process is furthered, albeit imperceptibly. Prayer is the discovery of Christ within – time spent solely in his presence in the quiet sanctuary of the heart. Because of the profound coinherence of all humanity, this place of loving becomes a fountain of intercession for all those with whom our lives are connected. In this way contemplation and intercession are two aspects of the same encounter with Christ. The heart becomes the sanctuary within which the presence of the Spirit may be sensed and the fire of his love kindled. This is the 'new and living way – the way of his flesh' which Christ has created at the heart of humanity, by which the threshold of the sanctuary of heaven itself may be approached (Heb. 10:20). Only through lives transformed in this arduous manner do true healing and vision come for the life of the church and the world.

The hidden heart of the church's life is found in the witness of her saints, of whom only a small sample are ever widely known in their lifetime, or thereafter. Central, therefore, to the true welfare and life of any church must be the search for sanctity. It was once asked by an Orthodox Christian of an Anglican, "Does your church produce saints?" To this the Anglican gave a cautious "Yes". "But does your church recognise and relate to its saints? Does it expect them to arise in your midst even now?" This was a more searching enquiry, to which the Anglican gave a more hesitant reply. It is a vital point.

Saints are those whose lives embody and mediate the reality in which they believe, whose characters communicate the pattern of living through dying, in whom the marks of Christ's passion may be discerned. Through them the Spirit is communicated in a life-transforming way, even after their deaths. Saints are generated by churches and traditions steeped in prayerful self-sacrifice. They arise in dialogue with the churches which nurtured them, even if during their lifetime that dialogue proved a stormy one. Their teaching also is in dialogue with faithful fellow-Christians who call forth, and can respond to and recall what they proclaim by word and deed. The reality of saints puts a very different light on the meaning of Christian history between the times of the New Testament and today. Their lives manifest for those with eyes to see what the Holy Spirit can achieve in human nature. The common pattern to their lives is Christlike, in compassion and prayer, in suffering and spiritual conflict. Yet this experience etches ever deeper the character of each unique personality. Their sanctity is confirmed by the reality of the resurrection and eternal life which breaks through their personalities both in their own times and subsequently, usually with healing consequences for others. In short, they are proof of the reality of the gospel of eternal life, obtained through participation in the dying and living of Christ which is accomplished by the power of the Holy Spirit within them. For as St Seraphim of Sarov once declared: 'to obtain the Holy Spirit is the goal of Christian life'. Thus a church which does not deliberately nurture and pray for sanctity of this kind is woefully impoverished in its own life, and tragically handicapped in its witness to the world.

The church exists to create the conditions in which the Holy Spirit can act. To achieve this vocation, it has first to secure the integrity of its worship and belief. This is the focus of its unity and that which determines its character and effectiveness. Crucial to this process is the integrity of language. In a free society, people will openly hold a range of views and beliefs inside a church. But it is important to be clear exactly what constitutes Christian belief, by which people who call themselves Christian should measure and mould their own thinking during the time of their personal pilgrimage of faith. It is certainly not right to declare as consistent with Christian belief an understanding which departs significantly from that which Christian tradition has always understood to be the meaning of, for example, the Creeds. The integrity and effectiveness of human language rests upon truthfulness, both of understanding and of intention. The integrity of the language of Christian belief rests also upon actual historical events interpreted in the light of divine self-revelation. The distinctive pattern of Christian words, in the New Testament and in the Creeds, constitutes the channel of divine truth by which we may enter in the end into all truth (cf. John 16:13). It is this principle which underlies how language is used in Christian worship.

To participate in the eucharist, or in the recital of the divine office, is to be drawn into an ancient and age-old pattern of life-giving language. It is to open the heart and mind to the action of the Holy Spirit, reaching out to man through the words of men who were in dialogue with God. It is not simply the communication of intellectual truth, or of emotional sensation. It is our response to the divine call to love God 'with all your heart, with all your soul, with all your mind, and with all your strength' (Mark 12:30). Worship becomes a life-transforming experience in which God, as it were, calls the tune. In every age, not least today, this is an abrupt challenge to the human desire for self-gratification and entertainment through worship. Instead, language is recovered in worship in its truly symbolic character, mediating the saving power of the realities it describes, making men and women participants in a divine action which transcends time and space, in the worship of the wider church and of the church in heaven. Worship can save people and lead them to faith and vision, because when its language is handled faithfully and in a sincere and disciplined way, Christian worshippers become themselves partakers and communicators of the divine love which reaches out to them and through them.

Fundamental to the life and witness of the church is also the integrity of its moral values. Christian morality expresses a vision of humanity in the light of divine love for man. It creates the conditions in which holiness may be experienced and achieved. In the midst of human misery, sin and moral perplexity, Christianity affirms and should demonstrate that there is solid ground towards which people may make their way safely. The sanctity of all human life from conception until natural death is the core of this solid ground. Then there is the central importance of marriage for determining human values and relationships across generations, and for eluci- dating the meaning of love and sexuality. This is found in chastity, by which Christians mean respect for the integrity of each person in their relationships at all levels. It is expressed by generous self-giving which respects both the gift and the receiver of that giving. Finally, there is the sovereignty of human freedom in response to divine truth, to which all relationships are subordinate. These are constituent parts of the solid ground of Christian morality and ethics, relevant and available to all human beings everywhere. Human freedom only becomes fully established in response to divine truth, and the character and purpose of that divine truth is love for mankind.

Upon this matter, Pope John Paul II has this to say in his encycli- cal *Veritatis Splendor*:

This essential bond between Truth, the Good and Freedom has been largely lost sight of by present-day culture. As a result, helping man to rediscover it represents nowadays one of the specific requirements of the Church's mission, for the salvation of the world. Pilate's question: 'What is truth?' reflects the distressing perplexity of a man who often no longer knows who he is, whence he comes or where he is going. Hence we not infrequently witness the fearful plunging of the human person into situations of gradual self-destruction. According to some, it appears that one no longer need acknowledge the enduring absoluteness of any moral value. All around us we encounter contempt for human life after conception and before birth; the ongoing violation of basic rights of the person; the unjust destruction of goods minimally necessary for a human life. Indeed, something more serious has happened: man is no longer convinced that only in the truth can he find salvation. The saving power of truth is contested, and freedom alone, uprooted from any objectivity, is left to decide by itself what is good and what is evil. This relativism becomes, in the field of theology, a lack of trust in the wisdom of God, who guides man with the moral law. Concrete situations are unfavourably contrasted with the precepts of the moral law, nor is it any longer maintained that, when all is said and done, the law of God is always the one true good of man. (p. 129)

St Paul challenges Christians to offer themselves, even in all their sinfulness and failure, as a living sacrifice, dedicated to God continually: 'Conform no longer to the pattern of this present world, but be transformed by the renewal of your minds. Then you will be able to discern the will of God, and to know what is good, acceptable and perfect' (Rom. 12:2). This process he has described as a living through dying, a painful and hard road stretching over a lifetime in which wrong attitudes are righted and addiction to sinful passions is eradicated, so that the love of God becomes the well-spring for true and life-giving love for other human beings. Jesus declared: 'If you stand by my teaching, you are truly my disciples; you will know the truth, and the truth will set you free' (John 8:31-32). What is the truth, and how can it set men free? Only the path of living through dying, the narrow and afflicted way to Calvary and beyond, will indicate how this transformation is achieved by God in a person's life. For as the Pope concludes in *Veritatis Splendor*:

> Jesus is the living, personal summation of perfect freedom in total obedience to the will of God. His crucified flesh fully reveals the unbreakable bond between freedom and truth, just as his Resurrection from the dead is the supreme exaltation of the fruitfulness and saving power of a freedom lived out in truth. (p. 134)

Thus the church cannot remain silent in the face of political and social actions and values which undermine human dignity and freedom. Natural to the church's nature and character is an unshakeable bond of solidarity which transcends all human barriers of nationality, race or class. Even at the risk of ridicule, contempt and persecution, Christians must fearlessly affirm the value of all human beings to God in both their individual and corporate lives. The Cross of Christ reveals the nature of the conflict between man and man, which began in Cain's killing of his brother Abel, and how evil is manipulating people against each other to such destructive ends. The light of the resurrection, the values of the eternal kingdom of God's love, pierce into the darkest corners of man's inhumanity to man. In many parts of the world the church is a suffering part of suffering humanity, in poverty or persecution. It is this bond of common suffering which, when united with that of Jesus on the Cross, turns outward in service and compassion, and in championing human rights against all manner of abuse and degradation. The church exists to demonstrate to mankind that we are all indeed members one of another, and that God's compassion embraces both the victims and the perpetrators of cruelty. For as St Paul declared and exemplified in his own ministry and suffering:

> [Christ] is himself our peace. Gentiles and Jews, he has made the two one, and in his own body of flesh and blood has broken down the barrier of enmity which separated them ... so as to create out of the two a single new humanity in himself, thereby

making peace ... through the cross, by which he killed the enmity. (Eph. 2:14-16)

It is upon the basis of so costly and powerful a reconciliation, expressed and experienced in a common baptism and celebrated and deepened in the eucharist, that he can conclude elsewhere: 'There is no such thing as Jew and Greek, slave and freeman, male and female; for you are all one person in Christ Jesus' (Gal. 3:28). The signs and bonds of this new communion between human persons are a tangible fellowship of 'faith expressing itself through love' (Gal. 5:6), forged by suffering and compassion experienced and shared. The hallmarks of this true *koinonia* are a common language of belief, a common morality and a common worship.

It follows, therefore, that at all times Christians should affirm, experience and deepen the essential unity which is at the heart of the church, but without in any way undermining the rich diversity of its life. For the diversity of Christianity through time and place does not signify division, let alone justify conflict or competition between churches. It is, rather, testimony to the manifold grace of God reaching out to the manifold needs of man. It is like the great tree of which Jesus spoke in the parable of the mustard seed (cf. Mark 4:30-32): a tree is not itself without its diverging branches. But it is one tree because of its common roots, the seed which gave it life, the strength of its supporting trunk, and the rising sap which enables it to bear fruit.

The roots of the church are in the faith of the Jews expressed in the Old Testament and the religious world from which Jesus and his earliest Jewish disciples emerged. To this faith, and to the people of this faith, Christians remain permanently indebted. The seed sown into the ground to die and to bear this rich harvest is of course the life, death and resurrection of Jesus, and the common trunk is found in the core of belief expressed in the New Testament and reiterated in the Creeds. It is the hidden life of the Spirit, the well of living water springing up within, which alone sustains the life of the church, and enables it to bear fruit, the fruit of the Spirit which is everywhere the same in its quality, if varied in its colour. Meanwhile, to experience worship and faith in a branch of the church not one's own is to see aspects of Christianity in a completely new light, and to return more deeply committed to that branch which first nurtured one's faith and where it is one's vocation to be. No one branch of the church can really claim to do full justice to every aspect and ramification of Christian belief, and even genuine ecumenical experience only affords an inkling of how things truly are. But the life of the church mirrors, upholds and transforms the unity of mankind in all its rich diversity and varied needs. It is a sign both to itself and to the world of God's love and purpose towards man.

This great tree is also a 'burning bush', for within its life, often in unexpected ways and persons, the presence of God may be sensed, and at times even seen. For the good news which Christianity proclaims by its very existence is that the God who made the universe and every human being can be known and loved in a genuine way as Father. In the very darkest moments of human tragedy and pain, and in the very ordinariness of human relationships, God who became man in Jesus, the Son, may be served and met, for 'anything you did for one of my brothers here, however insignificant, you did for me' (cf. Matt. 25:40). There is, indeed, a deep purpose to human life, personal and corporate, and that purpose is revealed by the indwelling of the Holy Spirit who makes us truly the children of God. As a child once observed: 'Heaven is a very big place because it is where God is; but the way to it is very small because it is in our hearts'. Along this way, the way of living through dying, travel the saints, known and unknown, servants of God and of humanity in whom the reality of the divine Trinity, Father, Son and Holy Spirit, has come to dwell (cf. John 14:23-26).

To all human beings the voice of divine love calls from the heart of the life of the church:
Come for water, all who are thirsty;
though you have no money, come, buy grain and eat;
come, buy wine and milk, not for money, not for a price ...
Come to me and listen to my words, hear me and you will have life. (Isa. 55:1-3)
To a Samaritan woman, lost in herself and in relation to her own society, Christ proclaimed: 'whoever drinks the water I shall give him will never again be thirsty. The water that I shall give will be a spring of water within him, welling up and bringing eternal life'

(John 4:14). To those who truly follow him, he promises: 'If anyone is thirsty, let him come to me and drink. Whoever believes in me, as scripture says, 'Streams of living water shall flow from within him' (John 7:37-38). The evangelist points immediately to the Cross as the key to this outpouring of God's Spirit, for from the dead body of Christ flowed the blood and water (John 19:34), the costly sign that this was indeed the life-giver: 'This is he whose coming was with water and blood: Jesus Christ ... and to this the Spirit bears witness, because the Spirit is truth' (1 John 5:6). For St Paul also, Christ was 'the rock' which accompanied Israel of old through its exodus, from whom they drank and lived (cf. 1 Cor. 10:4). The final vision of the Bible is of the 'river of the water of life' at the heart of the city of God. To this city all are bidden, 'to accept the water of life as a gift' (Rev. 22:1-2, 17).

The Second Letter of Paul to the CORINTHIANS

1. FROM Paul, apostle of Christ Jesus by God's will, and our colleague Timothy, to God's church at Corinth, together with all God's people throughout the whole of Achaia.

²Grace and peace to you from God our Father and the Lord Jesus Christ.

³Praise be to the God and Father of our Lord Jesus Christ, the all-merciful Father, the God whose consolation never fails us! ⁴He consoles us in all our troubles, so that we in turn may be able to console others in any trouble of theirs and to share with them the consolation we ourselves receive from God. ⁵As Christ's suffering exceeds all measure and extends to us, so too it is through Christ that our consolation has no limit. ⁶If distress is our lot, it is the price we pay for your consolation and your salvation; if our lot is consolation, it is to help us to bring you consolation, and strength to face with fortitude the same sufferings we now endure. ⁷And our hope for you is firmly grounded; for we know that if you share in the suffering, you share also in the consolation.

⁸In saying this, my friends, we should like you to know how serious was the trouble that came upon us in the province of Asia. The burden of it was far too heavy for us to bear, so heavy that we even despaired of life. ⁹Indeed, we felt in our hearts that we had received a death sentence. This was meant to teach us to place reliance not on ourselves, but on God who raises the dead. ¹⁰From such mortal peril God delivered us; and he will deliver us again, he on whom our hope is fixed. Yes, he will continue to deliver us, ¹¹while you co-operate by praying for us. Then, with so many people praying for our deliverance, there will be many to give thanks on our behalf for God's gracious favour towards us.

Paul's concern for the church at Corinth

¹²THERE is one thing we are proud of: our conscience shows us that in our dealings with others, and above all in our dealings with you, our conduct has been governed by a devout and godly sincerity, by the grace of God and not by worldly wisdom. ¹³⁻¹⁴There is nothing in our letters to

you but what you can read and understand. You do understand us in some measure, but I hope you will come to understand fully that you have as much reason to be proud of us, as we of you, on the day of our Lord Jesus.

[15]It was because I felt so confident about all this that I had intended to come first of all to you and give you the benefit of a double visit: [16]I meant to visit you on my way to Macedonia and, after leaving Macedonia, to return to you, and you could then have sent me on my way to Judaea. [17]That was my intention; did I lightly change my mind? Or do I, when framing my plans, frame them as a worldly man might, first saying 'Yes, yes' and then 'No, no'? [18]God is to be trusted, and therefore what we tell you is not a mixture of Yes and No. [19]The Son of God, Christ Jesus, proclaimed among you by us (by Silvanus and Timothy, I mean, as well as myself), was not a mixture of Yes and No. With him it is always Yes; [20]for all the promises of God have their Yes in him. That is why, when we give glory to God, it is through Christ Jesus that we say 'Amen'. [21]And if you and we belong to Christ, guaranteed as his and anointed, it is all God's doing; [22]it is God also who has set his seal upon us and, as a pledge of what is to come, has given the Spirit to dwell in our hearts.

[23]I appeal to God as my witness and stake my life upon it: it was out of consideration for you that I did not after all come to Corinth. [24]It is not that we have control of your faith; rather we are working with you for your happiness. For it is by that faith that you stand.

2. [1]SO I made up my mind that my next visit to you must not be another painful one. [2]If I cause pain to you, who is left to cheer me up, except you whom I have offended? [3]This is precisely the point I made in my letter: I did not want, I said, to come and be made miserable by the very people who ought to have made me happy; and I had sufficient confidence in you all to know that for me to be happy is for all of you to be happy. [4]That letter I sent you came out of great distress and anxiety; how many tears I shed as I wrote it! Not because I wanted to cause you pain; rather I wanted you to know the love, the more than ordinary love, that I have for you.

[5]Any injury that has been done has not been done to me; to some extent (I do not want to make too much of it) it has been done to you all. [6]The penalty on which the general meeting has agreed has met the offence well enough. [7]Something very different is called for now: you must forgive the offender and put heart into him; the man's distress must not be made so severe as to overwhelm him. [8]I urge you therefore to reassure him of your love for him. [9]I wrote, I may say, to see how you stood the test, whether you fully accepted my authority. [10]But anyone who has your forgiveness has mine too; and when I speak of forgiving (so far as there is anything for

me to forgive), I mean that as the representative of Christ I have forgiven him for your sake. [11]For Satan must not be allowed to get the better of us; we know his wiles all too well.

[12]When I came to Troas, where I was to preach the gospel of Christ, and where an opening awaited me for serving the Lord, [13]I still found no relief of mind, for my colleague Titus was not there to meet me; so I took leave of the people and went off to Macedonia. [14]But thanks be to God, who continually leads us as captives in Christ's triumphal procession, and uses us to spread abroad the fragrance of the knowledge of himself! [15]We are indeed the incense offered by Christ to God, both among those who are on the way to salvation, and among those who are on the way to destruction: [16]to the latter it is a deadly fume that kills, to the former a vital fragrance that brings life. Who is equal to such a calling? [17]We are not adulterating the word of God for profit as so many do; when we declare the word we do it in sincerity, as from God and in God's sight, as members of Christ.

Paul's commission as an apostle

3. ARE we beginning all over again to produce our credentials? Do we, like some people, need letters of introduction to you, or from you? [2]No, you are all the letter we need, a letter written on our heart; anyone can see it for what it is and read it for himself. [3]And as for you, it is plain that you are a letter that has come from Christ, given to us to deliver; a letter written not with ink but with the Spirit of the living God, written not on stone tablets but on the pages of the human heart.

[4]It is in full reliance upon God, through Christ, that we make such claims. [5]There is no question of our having sufficient power in ourselves: we cannot claim anything as our own. The power we have comes from God; [6]it is he who has empowered us as ministers of a new covenant, not written but spiritual; for the written law condemns to death, but the Spirit gives life.

[7]The ministry that brought death, and that was engraved in written form on stone, was inaugurated with such glory that the Israelites could not keep their eyes on Moses, even though the glory on his face was soon to fade. [8]How much greater, then, must be the glory of the ministry of the Spirit! [9]If glory accompanied the ministry that brought condemnation, how much richer in glory must be the ministry that brings acquittal! [10]Indeed, the glory that once was is now no glory at all; it is outshone by a still greater glory. [11]For if what was to fade away had its glory, how much greater is the glory of what endures!

[12]With such a hope as this we speak out boldly; [13]it is not for us to do as

Moses did: he put a veil over his face to keep the Israelites from gazing at the end of what was fading away. [14]In any case their minds had become closed, for that same veil is there to this very day when the lesson is read from the old covenant; and it is never lifted, because only in Christ is it taken away. [15]Indeed to this very day, every time the law of Moses is read, a veil lies over the mind of the hearer. [16]But (as scripture says) 'Whenever he turns to the Lord the veil is removed.' [17]Now the Lord of whom this passage speaks is the Spirit; and where the Spirit of the Lord is, there is liberty. [18]And because for us there is no veil over the face, we all see as in a mirror the glory of the Lord, and we are being transformed into his likeness with ever-increasing glory, through the power of the Lord who is the Spirit.

4. SINCE God in his mercy has given us this ministry, we never lose heart. [2]We have renounced the deeds that people hide for very shame; we do not practise cunning or distort the word of God. It is by declaring the truth openly that we recommend ourselves to the conscience of our fellow-men in the sight of God. [3]If our gospel is veiled at all, it is veiled only for those on the way to destruction; [4]their unbelieving minds are so blinded by the god of this passing age that the gospel of the glory of Christ, who is the image of God, cannot dawn upon them and bring them light. [5]It is not ourselves that we proclaim; we proclaim Christ Jesus as Lord, and ourselves as your servants for Jesus's sake. [6]For the God who said, 'Out of darkness light shall shine,' has caused his light to shine in our hearts, the light which is knowledge of the glory of God in the face of Jesus Christ.

[7]But we have only earthenware jars to hold this treasure, and this proves that such transcendent power does not come from us; it is God's alone. [8]We are hard pressed, but never cornered; bewildered, but never at our wit's end; [9]hunted, but never abandoned to our fate; struck down, but never killed. [10]Wherever we go we carry with us in our body the death that Jesus died, so that in this body also the life that Jesus lives may be revealed. [11]For Jesus's sake we are all our life being handed over to death, so that the life of Jesus may be revealed in this mortal body of ours. [12]Thus death is at work in us, but life in you.

[13]But scripture says, 'I believed, and therefore I spoke out,' and we too, in the same spirit of faith, believe and therefore speak out; [14]for we know that he who raised the Lord Jesus to life will with Jesus raise us too, and bring us to his presence, and you with us. [15]Indeed, all this is for your sake, so that, as the abounding grace of God is shared by more and more, the greater may be the chorus of thanksgiving that rises to the glory of God.

[16]No wonder we do not lose heart! Though our outward humanity is in

decay, yet day by day we are inwardly renewed. [17]Our troubles are slight and short-lived, and their outcome is an eternal glory which far outweighs them, [18]provided our eyes are fixed, not on the things that are seen, but on the things that are unseen; for what is seen is transient, what is unseen is eternal.

5. [1]WE know that if the earthly frame that houses us today is demolished, we possess a building which God has provided - a house not made by human hands, eternal and in heaven. [2]In this present body we groan, yearning to be covered by our heavenly habitation put on over this one, [3]in the hope that, being thus clothed, we shall not find ourselves naked. [4]We groan indeed, we who are enclosed within this earthly frame; we are oppressed because we do not want to have the old body stripped off. What we want is to be covered by the new body put on over it, so that our mortality may be absorbed into life immortal. [5]It is for this destiny that God himself has been shaping us; and as a pledge of it he has given us the Spirit.

[6]Therefore we never cease to be confident. We know that so long as we are at home in the body we are exiles from the Lord; [7]faith is our guide, not sight. [8]We are confident, I say, and would rather be exiled from the body and make our home with the Lord. [9]That is why it is our ambition, wherever we are, at home or in exile, to be acceptable to him. [10]For we must all have our lives laid open before the tribunal of Christ, where each must receive what is due to him for his conduct in the body, good or bad.

The message of reconciliation

[11]WITH this fear of the Lord before our eyes we address our appeal to men and women. To God our lives lie open, and I hope that in your heart of hearts they lie open to you also. [12]This is not another attempt to recommend ourselves to you: we are rather giving you a chance to show yourselves proud of us; then you will have something to say to those whose pride is all in outward show and not in inward worth. [13]If these are mad words, take them as addressed to God; if sound sense, as addressed to you. [14]For the love of Christ controls us once we have reached the conclusion that one man died for all and therefore all mankind has died. [15]He died for all so that those who live should cease to live for themselves, and should live for him who for their sake died and was raised to life. [16]With us therefore worldly standards have ceased to count in our estimate of anyone; even if once they counted in our understanding of Christ, they do so now no longer. [17]For anyone united to Christ, there is a new creation: the old order has gone; a new order has already begun.

[18]All this has been the work of God. He has reconciled us to himself through Christ, and has enlisted us in this ministry of reconciliation: [19]God was in Christ reconciling the world to himself, no longer holding people's misdeeds against them, and has entrusted us with the message of reconciliation. [20]We are therefore Christ's ambassadors. It is as if God were appealing to you through us: we implore you in Christ's name, be reconciled to God! [21]Christ was innocent of sin, and yet for our sake God made him one with human sinfulness, so that in him we might be made one with the righteousness of God.

6. [1]Sharing in God's work, we make this appeal: you have received the grace of God; do not let it come to nothing. [2]He has said:

In the hour of my favour I answered you; on the day of deliverance
I came to your aid.
This is the hour of favour, this the day of deliverance.

[3]Lest our ministry be brought into discredit, we avoid giving any offence in anything. [4]As God's ministers, we try to recommend ourselves in all circumstances by our steadfast endurance: in affliction, hardship, and distress; [5]when flogged, imprisoned, mobbed; overworked, sleepless, starving. [6]We recommend ourselves by innocent behaviour and grasp of truth, by patience and kindliness, by gifts of the Holy Spirit, by unaffected love, [7]by declaring the truth, by the power of God. We wield the weapons of righteousness in right hand and left. [8]Honour and dishonour, praise and blame, are alike our lot: we are the impostors who speak the truth, [9]the unknown men whom all men know; dying we still live on; disciplined by suffering, we are not done to death; [10]in our sorrows we have always cause for joy; poor ourselves, we bring wealth to many; penniless, we own the world.

[11]We have spoken very frankly to you, friends in Corinth; we have opened our heart to you. [12]There is no constraint on our part; any constraint there may be is in you. [13]In fair exchange then (if I may speak to you like a father) open your hearts to us.

Church life and discipline

[14]DO NOT team up with unbelievers. What partnership can righteousness have with wickedness? Can light associate with darkness? [15]Can Christ agree with Belial, or a believer join with an unbeliever? [16]Can there be a compact between the temple of God and idols? And the temple of the living God is what we are. God's own words are: 'I will live and move about among them; I will be their God, and they shall be my people.' [17]And

therefore, 'Come away and leave them, separate yourselves, says the Lord; touch nothing unclean. Then I will accept you, [18]says the Lord Almighty; I will be a father to you, and you shall be my sons and daughters.'

7. [1]SUCH are the promises that have been made to us, dear friends. Let us therefore cleanse ourselves from all that can defile flesh or spirit and, in the fear of God, let us complete our consecration.

[2]MAKE a place for us in your hearts! We have wronged no one, ruined no one, exploited no one. [3]My words are no reflection on you. I have told you before that, come death, come life, your place in our hearts is secure. [4]I am speaking to you with great frankness, but my pride in you is just as great. In all our many troubles my cup is full of consolation and overflows with joy.

[5]Even when we reached Macedonia we still found no relief; instead trouble met us at every turn, fights without and fears within. [6]But God, who brings comfort to the downcast, has comforted us by the arrival of Titus, [7]and not merely by his arrival, but by his being so greatly encouraged about you. He has told us how you long for me, how sorry you are, and how eager to take my side; and that has made me happier still.

[8]Even if I did hurt you by the letter I sent, I do not now regret it. I did regret it; but now that I see the letter gave you pain, though only for a time, [9]I am happy - not because of the pain but because the pain led to a change of heart. You bore the pain as God would have you bear it, and so you came to no harm from what we did. [10]Pain borne in God's way brings no regrets but a change of heart leading to salvation; pain borne in the world's way brings death. [11]You bore your pain in God's way, and just look at the results: it made you take the matter seriously and vindicate yourselves; it made you indignant and apprehensive; it aroused your longing for me, your devotion, and your eagerness to see justice done! At every point you have cleared yourselves of blame. [12]And so, although I did send you that letter, it was not the offender or his victim that most concerned me. My aim in writing was to help to make plain to you, in the sight of God, how truly you are devoted to us. [13]That is why we have been so encouraged.

But besides being encouraged ourselves, we have also been delighted beyond everything by seeing how happy Titus is: you have all helped to set his mind completely at rest. [14]Anything I may have said to him to show my pride in you has been justified. Every word we addressed to you bore the mark of truth, and the same holds of the proud boast we made in the presence of Titus; that also has proved true. [15]His heart warms all the more to you as he recalls how ready you all were to do what he asked, meeting him as you did in fear the trembling. [16]How happy I am now to have complete confidence in you!

The collection for the church in Jerusalem

8. WE must tell you, friends, about the grace that God has given to the churches in Macedonia. [2]The troubles they have been through have tried them hard, yet in all this they have been so exuberantly happy that from the depths of their poverty they have shown themselves lavishly open-handed. [3]Going to the limit of their resources, as I can testify, and even beyond that limit, [4]they begged us most insistently, and on their own initiative, to be allowed to share in this generous service to their fellow-Christians. [5]And their giving surpassed our expectations; for first of all they gave themselves to the Lord and, under God, to us. [6]The upshot is that we have asked Titus, since he has already made a beginning, to bring your share in this further work of generosity also to completion. [7]You are so rich in everything - in faith, speech, knowledge, and diligence of every kind, as well as in the love you have for us - that you should surely show yourselves equally lavish in this generous service! [8]This is not meant as an order; by telling you how keen others are I am putting your love to the test. [9]You know the generosity of our Lord Jesus Christ: he was rich, yet for your sake he became poor, so that through his poverty you might become rich.

[10]Here is my advice, and I have your interests at heart. You made a good beginning last year both in what you did and in your willingness to do it. [11]Now go on and finish it. Be as eager to complete the scheme as you were to adopt it, and give according to your means. [12]If we give eagerly according to our means, that is acceptable to God; he does not ask for what we do not have. [13]There is no question of relieving others at the cost of hardship to yourselves; [14]it is a question of equality. At the moment your surplus meets their need, but one day your need may be met from their surplus. The aim is equality; [15]as scripture has it, 'Those who gathered more did not have too much, and those who gathered less did not have too little.'

[16]I thank God that he has made Titus as keen on your behalf as we are! [17]So keen is he that he not only welcomed our request; it is by his own choice he is now leaving to come to you. [18]With him we are sending one of our company whose reputation for his services to the gospel among all the churches is high. [19]Moreover they have duly appointed him to travel with us and help in this beneficent work, by which we do honour to the Lord himself and show our own eagerness to serve. [20]We want to guard against any criticism of our handling of these large sums; [21]for our aims are en-

tirely honourable, not only in the Lord's eyes, but also in the eyes of men and women.

²²We are sending with them another of our company whose enthusiasm we have had repeated opportunities of testing, and who is now all the more keen because of the great confidence he has in you. ²³If there is any question about Titus, he is my partner and my fellow-worker in dealing with you; as for the others, they are delegates of the churches and bring honour to Christ. ²⁴So give them, and through them the churches, clear evidence of your love and justify our pride in you.

9. ABOUT this aid for God's people, it is superfluous for me to write to you. ²I know how eager you are to help and I speak of it with pride to the Macedonians, telling them that Achaia had everything ready last year; and most of them have been fired by your zeal. ³My purpose in sending these friends is to ensure that what we have said about you in this matter should not prove to be an empty boast. I want you to be prepared, as I told them you were; ⁴for if I bring men from Macedonia with me and they find you are not prepared, what a disgrace it will be to us, let alone to you, after all the confidence we have shown! ⁵I have accordingly thought it necessary to ask these friends to go on ahead to Corinth, to see that your promised bounty is in order before I come; it will then be awaiting me as genuine bounty, and not as an extortion.

⁶Remember: sow sparingly, and you will reap sparingly; sow bountifully, and you will reap bountifully. ⁷Each person should give as he has decided for himself; there should be no reluctance, no sense of compulsion; God loves a cheerful giver. ⁸And it is in God's power to provide you with all good gifts in abundance, so that, with every need always met to the full, you may have something to spare for every good cause; ⁹as scripture says: 'He lavishes his gifts on the needy; his benevolence lasts for ever.' ¹⁰Now he who provides seed for sowing and bread for food will provide the seed for you to sow; he will multiply it and swell the harvest of your benevolence, ¹¹and you will always be rich enough to be generous. Through our action such generosity will issue in thanksgiving to God, ¹²for as a piece of willing service this is not only a contribution towards the needs of God's people; more than that, it overflows in a flood of thanksgiving to God. ¹³For with the proof which this aid affords, those who receive it will give honour to God when they see how humbly you obey him and how faithfully you confess the gospel of Christ; and they will thank him for your liberal contribution to their need and to the general good. ¹⁴And as they join in prayer on your behalf, their hearts will go out to you because of the richness of the grace which God has given you. ¹⁵Thanks be

to God for his gift which is beyond all praise!

The challenge to Paul's authority

10. I, PAUL, appeal to you by the gentleness and magnanimity of Christ - I who am so timid (you say) when face to face with you, so courageous when I am away from you. ²Spare me when I come, I beg you, the need for that courage and self-assurance, which I reckon I could confidently display against those who assume my behaviour to be dictated by human weakness. ³Weak and human we may be, but that does not dictate the way we fight our battles. ⁴The weapons we wield are not merely human; they are strong enough with God's help to demolish strongholds. ⁵We demolish sophistries and all that rears its proud head against the knowledge of God; we compel every human thought to surrender in obedience to Christ; ⁶and we are prepared to punish any disobedience once your own obedience is complete.

⁷Look facts in the face. Is someone convinced that he belongs to Christ? Let him think again and reflect that we belong to Christ as much as he does. ⁸Indeed, if I am boasting too much about our authority - an authority given by the Lord to build your faith, not pull it down - I shall make good my boast. ⁹So you must not think of me as one who tries to scare you by the letters he writes. ¹⁰'His letters', so it is said, 'are weighty and power-ful; but when he is present he is unimpressive, and as a speaker he is beneath contempt.' ¹¹People who talk in that way should reckon with this: my actions when I come will show the same man as my letters showed while I was absent.

¹²We should not dare to class ourselves or compare ourselves with any of those who commend themselves. What fools they are to measure them-selves on their own, to find in themselves their standard of comparison! ¹³As for us, our boasting will not go beyond the proper limits; and our sphere is determined by the limit God laid down for us, which permitted us to come as far as Corinth. ¹⁴We are not overstretching our commission, as we would be if we had never come to you; but we were the first to reach as far as Corinth in the work of the gospel of Christ. ¹⁵And we do not boast of work done where others have laboured, work beyond our proper sphere. Our hope is rather that, as your faith grows, we may attain a position among you greater than ever before, but still within the limits of our sphere. ¹⁶Then we can carry the gospel to lands that lie beyond you, never priding ourselves on work already done in anyone else's sphere. ¹⁷If anyone would boast, let him boast of the Lord. ¹⁸For it is not the one who recommends himself, but the one whom the Lord recommends, who is to be accepted.

Paul speaks as a fool

11. I SHOULD like you to bear with me in a little foolishness; please bear with me. [2]I am jealous for you, with the jealousy of God; for I betrothed you to Christ, thinking to present you as a chaste virgin to her true and only husband. [3]Now I am afraid that, as the serpent in his cunning seduced Eve, your thoughts may be corrupted and you may lose your single-hearted devotion to Christ. [4]For if some newcomer proclaims another Jesus, not the Jesus whom we proclaimed, or if you receive a spirit different from the Spirit already given to you, or a gospel different from the gospel you have already accepted, you put up with that well enough. [5]I am not aware of being in any way inferior to those super-apostles. [6]I may be no speaker, but knowledge I do have; at all times we have made known to you the full truth.

[7]Or was this my offence, that I made no charge for preaching the gospel of God, humbling myself in order to exalt you? [8]I robbed other churches - by accepting support from them to serve you. [9]If I ran short while I was with you, I did not become a charge on anyone; my needs were fully met by friends from Macedonia; I made it a rule, as I always shall, never to be a burden to you. [10]As surely as the truth of Christ is in me, nothing shall bar me from boasting about this throughout Achaia. [11]Why? Because I do not love you? God knows I do.

[12]And I shall go on doing as I am doing now, to cut the ground from under those who would seize any chance to put their vaunted apostleship on the same level as ours. [13]Such people are sham apostles, confidence tricksters masquerading as apostles of Christ. [14]And no wonder! Satan himself masquerades as an angel of light, [15]so it is easy enough for his agents to masquerade as agents of good. But their fate will match their deeds.

[16]I repeat: let no one take me for a fool; but if you must, then give me the privilege of a fool, and let me have my little boast like others. [17]In boasting so confidently I am not speaking like a Christian, but like a fool. [18]So many people brag of their earthly distinctions that I shall do so too. [19]How gladly you put up with fools, being yourselves so wise! [20]If someone tyrannizes over you, exploits you, gets you in his clutches, puts on airs, and hits you in the face, you put up with it. [21]And you call me a weakling! I admit the reproach.

But if there is to be bravado (and I am still speaking as a fool), I can indulge in it too. [22]Are they Hebrews? So am I. Israelites? So am I. Abraham's descendants? So am I. [23]Are they servants of Christ? I am mad to speak like this, but I can outdo them: more often overworked, more often imprisoned, scourged more severely, many a time face to face with death. ²⁴Five times the Jews have given me the thirty-nine strokes; ²⁵three times I have been beaten with rods; once I was stoned; three times I have been shipwrecked, and for twenty-four hours I was adrift on the open sea. ²⁶I have been constantly on the road; I have met dangers from rivers, dangers from robbers, dangers from my fellow-countrymen, dangers from foreigners, dangers in the town, dangers in the wilderness, dangers at sea, dangers from false Christians. ²⁷I have toiled and drudged and often gone without sleep; I have been hungry and thirsty and have often gone without food; I have suffered from cold and exposure.

²⁸Apart from these external things, there is the responsibility that weighs on me every day, my anxious concern for all the churches. ²⁹Is anyone weak? I share his weakness. If anyone brings about the downfall of another, does my heart not burn with anger? ³⁰If boasting there must be, I will boast of the things that show up my weakness. ³¹He who is blessed for ever, the God and Father of the Lord Jesus, knows that what I say is true. ³²When I was in Damascus, the commissioner of King Aretas kept the city under observation to have me arrested; ³³and I was let down in a basket, through a window in the wall, and so escaped his clutches.

12. IT may do no good, but I must go on with my boasting; I come now to visions and revelations granted by the Lord. ²I know a Christian man who fourteen years ago (whether in the body or out of the body, I do not know - God knows) was caught up as far as the third heaven. ³And I know that this same man (whether in the body or apart from the body, I do not know - God knows) ⁴was caught up into paradise, and heard words so secret that human lips may not repeat them. ⁵About such a man I am ready to boast; but I will not boast on my own account, except of my weaknesses. ⁶If I chose to boast, it would not be the boast of a fool, for I should be speaking the truth. But I refrain, because I do not want anyone to form an estimate of me which goes beyond the evidence of his own eyes and ears. ⁷To keep me from being unduly elated by the magnificence of such revelations, I was given a thorn in my flesh, a messenger of Satan sent to buffet me; this was to save me from being unduly elated. ⁸Three times I begged the Lord to rid me of it, ⁹but his answer was: 'My grace is all you need; power is most fully seen in weakness.' I am therefore happy to boast of my weaknesses, because then the power of Christ will rest upon me. ¹⁰So I am content with a life of weakness, insult, hardship, persecution, and distress, all for Christ's sake; for when I am weak, then I am strong.

Paul's final appeal

¹¹I AM being very foolish, but it was you who drove me to it; my credentials

should have come from you. In nothing did I prove inferior to those super-apostles, even if I am a nobody. [12]The signs of an apostle were there in the work I did among you, marked by unfailing endurance, by signs, portents, and miracles. [13]Is there any way in which you were treated worse than the other churches - except this, that I was never a charge on you? Forgive me for being so unfair!

[14]I am now getting ready to pay you a third visit; and I am not going to be a charge on you. It is you I want, not your money; parents should make provision for their children, not children for their parents. [15]I would gladly spend everything for you - yes, and spend myself to the limit. If I love you overmuch, am I to be loved the less? [16]All very well, you say; I did not myself prove a burden to you, but I did use a confidence trick to take you in. [17]Was it one of the men I sent to you that I used to exploit you? [18]I begged Titus to visit you, and I sent our friend with him. Did Titus exploit you? Have we not both been guided by the same Spirit, and followed the same course?

[19]Perhaps you have been thinking all this time that it is to you we are addressing our defence. No; we are speaking in God's sight, and as Christians. Our whole aim, dear friends, is to build you up. [20]I fear that when I come I may find you different from what I wish, and you may find me to be what you do not wish. I fear I may find quarrelling and jealousy, angry tempers and personal rivalries, backbiting and gossip, arrogance and general disorder. [21]I am afraid that when I come my God may humiliate me again in your presence, that I may have cause to grieve over many who were sinning before and have not repented of their unclean lives, their fornication and sensuality.

13. This will be my third visit to you. As scripture says, 'Every charge must be established on the evidence of two or three witnesses': [2]to those who sinned before, and to everyone else, I repeat the warning I gave last time; on my second visit I gave it in person, and now I give it while absent. It is that when I come this time, I will show no leniency. [3]Then you will have the proof you seek of the Christ who speaks through me, the Christ who, far from being weak with you, makes his power felt among you. [4]True, he died on the cross in weakness, but he lives by the power of God; so you will find that we who share his weakness shall live with him by the power of God.

[5]Examine yourselves: are you living the life of faith? Put yourselves to the test. Surely you recognize that Jesus Christ is among you? If not, you have failed the test. [6]I hope you will come to see that we have not failed. [7]Our prayer to God is that you may do no wrong, not that we should win

approval; we want you to do what is right, even if we should seem failures. [8]We have no power to act against the truth, but only for it. [9]We are happy to be weak at any time if only you are strong. Our prayer, then, is for your amendment. [10]In writing this letter before I come, my aim is to spare myself, when I do come, any sharp exercise of authority - authority which the Lord gave me for building up and not for pulling down.

[11]And now, my friends, farewell. Mend your ways; take our appeal to heart; agree with one another; live in peace; and the God of love and peace will be with you. [12]Greet one another with the kiss of peace. [13]All God's people send you greetings.

[14]The grace of the Lord Jesus Christ, and the love of God, and the fellowship of the Holy Spirit, be with you all.

Index of Biblical References

Old Testament

New Testament